Tour Round the World.

SKETCHES

OF A

TOUR ROUND THE WORLD.

BY

P. C. MOZOOMDAR.

𝕮𝖆𝖑𝖈𝖚𝖙𝖙𝖆 :

S. K. Lahiri & Co.
BOOK:SELLERS & PUBLISHERS,

1884.

PRINNTED BY CHARU KANTI SANYAL
HARE PRESS, 14, COLLEGE SQUARE, CALCUTTA.
PUBLISHED BY S. K. LAHIRI & CO.
54, COLLEGE STREET, CALCUTTA.

PREFACE.

I feel some hesitation in offering these pages to the public. When I returned from my tour last January, I had no idea of publishing a book. It is due entirely to the good will and enterprise of the publishers that these sketches appear in their present shape. But I cannot help the feeling that neither in manner nor in matter the little book is what it ought to be. In a rapid tour of ten months I had only time, among other engagements, to draw some hurried sketches of scenes, events, and individuals that fell in my way. A few of these have already appeared in detached forms, and have been so far well received. But whether the others which by far form the larger number, will meet with the like approval I do not know. In any case I shall have to depend a good deal on the indulgence of the public. The superficialities of a hasty sojourner might perhaps meet with lenient criticism from the experience of the better informed. While it is to be hoped that such way-side pictures as I have tried to give, whatever may be their real worth, would call forth some real interest among my young country men who are fast imbibing a taste for foreign travel.

PEACE COTTAGE,
CALCUTTA, SEPTR. 1884. } P. C. M.

CONTENTS:—

	Page.
Preface.	
How the Hindu Travels	1
Ceylon	7
From Colombo to Gibralter	12
Arrival in London	18
The City of London	24
May Meetings	25
The Anglo Indian at Home	27
India office	29
John Bright at breakfast	31
An English Political Festival	38
The Atlantic	47
The People of America	52
The Vastness of America	57
American Freedom	62
The Red Man	68
Negro Piety	73
Religion in America	80
The Falls of Niagra	85
The American Woman	90
American Newspapers	96

Emerson	103
President Arthur	110
Mrs. Stowe	115
Henry Ward Beecher	117
My Work in Great Britain	119
A Trip to Germany	132
Dean Stanley	138
Prof. Tyndall	141
F. W. Newman	145
Cardinal Newman	146
Max Müller	148
My Work in America	151
Through the Pacific to Japan	158
Who are the Japanese	163
The Religion of Japan	167
Japan Modernized	171
Jeddo or Tokio	183
Japanese Wisdom	191
The Chinese	195
Penang and Singapore	205
Table of operations in England	211
Table of operations in America	214
Table of distances travelled	217

HOW THE HINDU TRAVELS.

In considerable flurry and fear our mild Hindu reformer wends his way to the P. and O. Company's office in Calcutta, and submits to the ominous process of securing his passage. A cold trepidation seizes him at the bottom of the dingy stair-case, where mysterious packing cases and labels swim before his wandering eyes. He musters courage to approach the half-screened office door, on pushing which he suddenly stands revealed to a solemn heavy-visaged official, who looks doubly formidable for having cropped his iron-grey beard, as if for this particular emergency. But that cannot be. The reforming Hindu is scanned from head to foot. He ventures to suggest that he is going to England, and would like to secure his passage. "*You* go to England?" asks the impenetrable official, concentrating such an amount of emphasis on the personal pronoun, second person, that our friend finds a strong flavor of the Criminal Procedure Amendment Bill agitation infused involuntarily into his system. "Yes," he replies apparently unconcerned, "I am going to England." "What is your name?" At this moment a somewhat undersized English gentleman walks into the room, and takes a chair unbidden. The mild Hindu who remained standing all this time, is left to his own thoughts and resources, and the obliging official devotes his time, attention, and powers of persuasion to the person just arrived, offering him information about the voyage, showing him plans of the vessel about to leave, and giving him an option of cabins he might find most convenient. All this took a long while during which our friend had opportunity, if he had the wish, to indulge in unlimited meditation on the advantages of travelling, and the social amenities of the Criminal Procedure Amendment Bill. When the European customer had gone, the heavy-visaged official once more turned his cropped beard towards our mild friend, and asked, "Well, have you made up your mind?" He answered, "Yes, will you kindly give me a good berth?" "I will give you a forward cabin, or one on the hurricane deck." "Yes, but will that be comfortable?" "Ah, comfortable? I dare say it will be. Mr. Justice—, the Hon'ble Mrs.—do not object to take cabins on that deck, and I suppose what is good for them, will be good enough for you!" To an argument so overpowering what could our mild Aryan say? If there was any deficiency in the manners and sentiments of the benevolent official to carry absolute conviction to the tardy intellectual powers of the degenerate Hindu, the mention of the names of Justice———and Hon'ble Mrs.———more than made up for it. He produced his 680 Rs., secured his passage, and had his berth assigned to him. Only as he returned home he very much wondered where the hurricane deck was, and what he would have to do with the great personages whose names had been mentioned to overthrow his contumacy. He soon discovered to his cost that to be on the same *deck* with people meant very much as to be on the same *ship* with them. The honorables and others had been allotted airy little one-berth or two-berth cabins on the right side of the ship, while our mild Hindu friend, perhaps in deference to his national prejudice, had been placed in a hole with the cow-house on one side, and the slaughter-house on the other. Then it was that our friend put hand to his head, and reflected how in the case of all his countrymen who had gone to Europe before him, they had either been berthed before the furance of the engine, or put away next to the W. C., or, as in his own case, placed between the cattle-stall and the meat-stall. The money was all good Government money, no fault in that. The fault lay in the fact that Europeans did not like to associate with Hindus on boardship. And no place was too much out of the way for them.

Now let us suppose our friend has embarked. The ship is one of the largest owned by the Company. One formidable difficulty the Hindu traveller has to deal with lies in the diet supplied on board. It is said in America that the American eats to live, and the Englishman lives to eat. Be that as it may, the Hindu travelling to England finds that there is more eating both in quantity and in frequency amongst his fellow-passengers than his nature can stand. There are six meals on board beginning from half-past six in the morning, and lasting till about nine in the evening. Before you are fully awake the steward shakes you out of your slumbers, and in stentorian notes announces "Your tea Sir", and hands over to you a red-hot mixture of the color and taste of new-made bricks, and crumbs of biscuits as hard as German polysyllables. The real breakfast comes at half-past 8 o'clock. And on entering the saloon you find laid out before you a feast of carcasses in which bipeds and quadrupeds of every kind lie mingled in bewildering array. Like Simon Peter the mild Hindu exclaims " nothing unclean hath passed my mouth"—how shall I eat all this? But hunger knows no law. And he has to obey the apostolic law of eating what is laid before him. At one o'clock the bell strikes again. And before the lowing herd has stopped its bleating in his digestive regions, the poor Hindu has to go down and swallow other herds again. Thus from meal to meal, and tea to tea the days go their round.

There is a large number and variety of passengers on board. Your overworked business man with a tired look and heavy gait, smoking near the quarter deck with an abstracted pre-occupied air. Your self-important civilian on furlough, with his Madrasi Ayah, his languid aristocratic wife, his irrepressible multifarious babies that *will* mix with " all" children, vainly puts on an air of authority that has ceased here. There is your fine young man, come out to India to shoot, now returning home, who has formed trenchant opinions on the corruptibility of all Native officials, and the people of the country in general, in the learned leisure of his six months' shooting expedition. He is a bachelor, attentive to ladies as a race, and to some ladies in particular. He will be an authority to all men when he returns to England. There is your clergyman of the Establishment whom very few talk to, who barely gets permission to conduct an hour's service on Sunday morning which the first-class passengers consider a great bore. There are scores of your Anglo-Indian ladies, besatined, bejewelled, changing satins, jewels, and scents at every one of the numerous meals. Amongst all these our mild patriot stalks alone, unaddressed, uninterrogated, uninterrupted, but scanned, stared at, and inquired about by the secret police of passenger curiosity. He is like a ghost let loose from another world, walking in this for an appointed season. Eating, reading, walking, sitting, he is absolutely alone. An excommunicated object, at no time favorably viewed, now regarded through the fierce light of the Criminal Procedure Amendment Bill. Tired and sick at heart he throws himself down listlessly on his deck chair; he is dozing quietly. Suddenly the sweet tones of the fair Anglo-Indian lady jar in his ears. " Why does that man go to sleep so near the ladies?" Our friend starts, half opens his eyes, yawns, and goes to sleep more doggedly than ever. Such are some of the amenities of travelling to Europe.

CEYLON.

Two days' sail from Madras gives you a distant sight of the great cocoanut groves and cinnamon forests of that classical island, surmounted by a high gallery of green hills, and fringed by a coral beach over which the emerald waves pour their treasures. Ceylon is an island of exceeding beauty, equally celebrated in the annals of Hinduism and Buddhism. You know a good deal about Pt. de Galle where all lines of steamers formerly used to stop. But of late Galle has been given up on account of the difficulties of its harbour, and Colombo has taken its place. You are aware that Colombo is the chief town of Ceylon, being the place where the political, military, and ecclesiastical heads of the island all reside. The good Bishop, whom I knew before, offered me his hospitality, and conversed to me about the prospects and tendencies of the settlement. Colombo has a population of about 1,20,000 comprising mostly of Buddhists, though a large portion of them are Christians also, both of the Roman Catholic and Protestant persuasions. The place where I saw most of the people was the Kotahena temple where the Bishop very kindly directed me. There was a festival going on at the time I was in Colombo, that is the 20th March. An immense colossal figure of Goutama, in the mendicant's ochre garb, and in the posture known as *sayani* (reclining,) has been lately constructed, and the eyes, costing about a thousand rupees, are being put upon the great idol. Hundreds have gathered, women and men, the majority perhaps women, gaily dressed, picturesquely combed, brilliantly ornamented, and not showing the least shyness in the vast assembly. Two Sramans are reading out of the sacred books in Pali, the poor are being sumptuously fed in rice and sweetmeats, immense masses of ivory, horn, cocoanut flowers, leaves, white young cocoanuts, and lanterns are put up. Altogether the Kotahena temple has a mediæval, uncorrupted Hindu aspect, most refreshing after the garish imitation of European finery in modern Indian Pujahs and festivals. The high priest comes out to speak with me. He speaks a kind of broken Sanskrit, the meaning of which I am just able to gather. He tells me the name of the temple is Dwapad-Uttama-Vihara, the abode of the best of men. The priests are all simply attired, humble, harmless and pure-looking as Buddhistic priests always are. Comparing with them the Lamas of Thibet and Sikim whom I have seen in the Himalayas, stalwart men, voluminously clad, eating beef and pork, and drinking country liquors, or even the Bonzes of Japan, I am willing to decide that the priests of Ceylon retain, more than any others, the original simplicity and purity of the Buddhistic Sramans and Bhikshus. From the conversations I have had, and the observations I have made, there was no doubt left in my mind that if our missionaries of the Brahma Samaj thought it worth their while to travel to Ceylon, and take up their residence in Colombo, they could produce the greatest effect upon the people.

I decidedly prefer Colombo to Madras in point of social and religious importance. Ceylon being under a separate Government, and being altogether more compact, has incomparably superior educational and religious prospects. And then the climate of the place is simply excellent. The recent visit of an American gentleman in connection with "Theosophy," has proved beyond doubt that the inhabitants of Ceylon are not without large and substantial sympathies. That under proper leadership they are able to make great progress is to me beyond doubt. To theistic missionary workers I point Ceylon as a most promising field, and I hope they will take advantage of the suggestion. Let some enterprising apostle of the New Dispensation plant his banner at Colombo, and form that effective alliance of sympathy with the great Buddhistic community which in the remote future will produce spiritual consequences of the utmost importance. But one thing I must beg leave to point out. None but the most abstemious men will succeed in Buddhistic Ceylon. I have the pleasure to know a member of the local Civil Service by name Mr. Neville, who takes great interest in Brahminic and Buddhistic antiquities. He told me that a young Englishman as he was, he had to take to rigid vegetarianism in order to have the sympathy of the people, and ready access to temples and sacred records. He promised every aid and co-operation if any missionary of the Brahma Samaj would visit Ceylon for the welfare of the inhabitants of the island. I ask, will no one take advantage of such facilities and advantages ?

FROM COLOMBO TO GIBRALTER.

1,380 miles across the Indian Ocean will take you to Aden, a strange-looking mysterious place, composed of black, beetling rocks overlooking the sea. You do not discover a blade of grass in any direction; it is weird, unpeopled, dark, forbidding. It has hills piled over hills, a gallery of desolation, and presents a rough, bleak, and inhospitable shore. And yet by the transforming hand of Great Britain, the barren wilderness has been turned into a scene of peace and comfort. The first thing that strikes you as you reach Aden is the number of strange beings who swim around your ship. They are naked, howling, dark-skinned undergrown men, with large white teeth, wooly hair, reddened with lime, and scarcely any clothing at all. They swim on the sea with their hands and with their legs alternately, sometimes with one hand and one leg only, and in all attitudes, cry "ya! ya!"—they seem to be an enlarged edition of our Indian tad-pole. They are aquatic in their habits, as comfortable in water as out of it. Directly you throw a two-anna piece, the boy or man plunges right into the sea with a splash, leaving his frail tiny canoe to take care of itself, and in a moment or two rises to the surface again with the shining silver piece held fast in his teeth. These divers are an African race of Mahomedans called Somalis. But here you see also the copper-coloured Arab with fierce looks, the women scarcely less masculine; the Bedouin, a lean, determined-looking man holding the nose-strings of his patient camel. Aden has a scanty supply of water. Water is actually sold by the weight in shops. As you climb the hills you see great artificial reservoirs dug, which are filled once in every two or three years by rain-fall. In Aden there are numerous Parsis, Hindus and Jews, young and old, who keep shops, and ask at least three times the saleable value of their wares. You meet also stately Nubians, tall, fine men, ebony-complexioned and clad in flowing white, most dignified in their manners, whose presence recalls to mind the semi-mythological Pharoahs of Egyptian antiquity. The richest commodities in Aden are the ostrich egg and ostrich feathers.

We next proceeded to Suez, which is 1,300 miles from Aden through the Red Sea. Suez is a regular Arab city. The only conveyance there is the highly-caparisoned donkey. I rode ignominiously on the back of a donkey, and wandered from street to street. I was told, Suez was an ideal Arab town, but I found it a very different place indeed. The streets are narrow and full of dirt. The people are rude, insolent, and cunning. I was therefore glad to ride back to my ship.

The railway journey from Suez to Alexandria across the Shahara desert is an interesting experience, but the heat is unbearable. As we swept on through the fleeting sands it suggested strange associations of the sufferings of the wandering Israelites. There were swarms of flies, and fiery winds, giving one sore eyes and burning thirst. But you are here on classical ground, and as you reach the father of the rivers, the Nile, the hot blasts cease, and suddenly you catch a sweet perfume, stumps of grass appear and vegetation is on view, the desert is suddenly transformed into a garden, and the people you meet are prosperous and picturesque. At about 8 o'clock we reached Alexandria, an ancient place, celebrated for various reasons,—for its library, its history, its philosophy, its classical tombs, and its great founder. The Alexandria of today is not what it was formerly. It is now filled with the sweepings, the tagrag of all countries in Europe, a veritable den of rascaldom. Be careful not to listen to the persuasions of every dragoman you meet with in this place. It is low in morals and civilization owing to the enormous shipping which congregates there from all parts of the world. Low Greeks and scampish-looking Turks loaf about in fezcaps, indigenous beggars and Egyptian coster-mongers beseige you at the street corners, German bandmasters and Bohemean singing girls enliven the cafes, Italian and Spanish sailors hang about with knives in their belts, and the British Philistine lords it over all. What is true of Alexandria is true also of Port Said.

We next proceeded to Malta, a British possession, an interesting little island. It is situated on lofty rocks rising abruptly out of the sea, the white houses, turrets, steeples, trees and fortifications crowding the sky in a great mass of picturesque variety. "The highest point of Malta is seven hundred and fifty feet above sea level. There are not many trees visible excepting in the walled-in gardens of the wealthy Maltese; but, in such enclosures, oranges, lemons, figs, pomegranates, and dry apples flourish. The potatoes raised in the island are of the best, and its string beans, peas, and beets are not surpassed anywhere. Olives do well here, and grow wild. In short, it is a climate most favorable for vegetables and semitropical fruits and flowers. The pumpkins are high in color, but low in taste. A sawdust pudding would be as palatable as a Maltese pumpkin pie. The "fields" of the Maltese peasant are enclosed in stone walls, and will not average more than half an acre each. Two-thirds of the surface of Malta is rock, and the soil of these fields has mostly been "made." It takes a man's lifetime to change a rock floor into a fertile "farm," but the Maltese are patient and industrious. They love their island. They affectionately call it *Fior del Mondo*, or the Flower of the World." An interesting object in Malta is the house of the

Governor, famous for the relics of the knights of St. George. Here are kept the helmets, swords, plumes and accoutrements of the knights of the Middle Ages. We visited the celebrated convent of the Capucines, and were escorted by the father, a big man with a bare head, bushy beard, a rope round his waist, to the crypt of the chapel where we saw the embalmed corpses of the saints of the order, some of whom died fifty, and some a hundred years ago, all dressed in ecclesiastical garments, the unburied bones and skins of the monks evidencing the immortality of the spirit of the good and great. This is the way they perpetuate religious excellence in Malta.

From Malta, we went to Gibralter, the Aden of Europe. Gibralter is a high rock towering some 1,400 feet above the level of the sea, and studded with cannon. The rock is fortified and English soldiers are to be seen everywhere. Just beyond this rock is neutral ground, half English and half Spanish, and great is the contrast between the short and underfed Spanish soldier with his faded uniform, and the trim English redcoat with his well-handled moustache. Gibralter has little general interest.

ARRIVAL IN LONDON.

Since my arrival in London on the 19th of April, I have been so continuously absorbed in various engagements that it has not been possible to address my friends before this. I feel it is the more necessary to write something for all, inasmuch as I cannot write separately to each one of them, though I feel so many will be truly anxious to hear of my progress. My long voyage, except for a sudden attack of illness on board, was prosperous being not without profit either to body or mind., But when at last the tedious thirty-seven days drew to their end, and I saw the misty mountainous coast of Devon and Cornwall on the raw wet morning of the 18th April, I could not but give thanks to God and heave a sigh of relief. The spring verdure was mantling the high irregular landscape, but the sky above, and all things below had a damp watery ungenial look, with a farm house here, a factory there, and commercial buildings on the sea face. We battled up the darkening fog, the damp mist, the cold wind, and the pelting rain, rolling heavily with the swell and surf which often washed the decks. Many of our passengers left at Plymouth, going by train to their several destinations, saying affectionate good bye to each other. For me, a stranger and outcaste as I have been on board, there is neither welfare nor farewell. I have only to look back and before, to the marvellous Graciousness that environs me, and be at rest.

On the very next day my voyage was to end, London to reach, human society to regain, and warm activity to recommence. And as on Thursday the 19th we were nearing the Albert and Victoria Docks amidst the fleets and fortifications, the barges boats and steamers of the crowded Thames, a young Englishman jumped on to the main-deck with a message of welcome for me, and a commission to escort me to my temporary home. We proceeded by train to Liverpool Street whence we drove on to the hospitable doors of our valued friend, the Rev. Robert Spears. The kind-hearted lady of the house, my affectionate old friend and sister, stood smiling on the door step, the children were excited by running in and out to receive me. Robin, the youngest, a fat Englishman of three or four summers, with red cheeks, massive legs, canny laughing eyes, acted the porter, carrying one of the packages upstairs, while John and Mary, my friends of the former visit, came, and shyly shook hands with me. Thus they welcomed and received me home. Full three weeks have I been under this hospitable roof, and must now look for lodgings elsewhere. I do not hesitate to say that the utmost thanks of the Brahmo Somaj of India are due to the Rev. Robert Spears, and his family for the cordial reception and kind help they have rendered to me. My visits and introductions have now ended. I have paid my respects now to the representatives of different sects and parties, addressing in the meanwhile such assemblies and congregations as came in my way. Lord Northbook has most kindly given me important introductions, besides himself showing considerable interest and anxiety for Indian progress. One of the powerful members of Government, and a natural leader of society, his unabated good will to our country and cause must be to every one of us a matter of singular pleasure. Some of the great officials of India Office, like Sir Barrow Ellis and others, have been courteously helpful to me. Amongst the High Church clergy, Canon Liddon has been most cordial in his inquiries and hospitality. Canon Farrar also was very kind, and as representing what is known as the Broad Church, holds a good deal of common ground with us. His elevation to a Bishopric which is soon expected, must act forcibly towards the progress of sound and true religion. A most friendly reception by Mr. Stopford Brooke has given me valuable insight into the working of deep liberal thought in theology. Dr. Martineau and Dr. Sadler of Hampstead, the latter inviting me to occupy his pulpit, represent the Unitarians. They have been very kind, and Mr. Philip Wicksteed, who is virtually a Theist, was the first to invite me to preach for him. Dr. Clarke, the Editor of the *Christian World*, a distinguished congregationalist gentleman, Dr. Davidson of the same denomination, have been present to meet me in the house of the late Mr. Samuel Sharpe, the great Egyptologist, and Hebrew scholar. The principal leaders of the English Jewish community, Dr. Marks, Messrs. Mocatta, Magnus and others, have given me a very cordial reception, and I hope before long to see the leading scientific men of England. But no word of cheer has been more cordial than that of Max Muller, our old well-tried friend. " You may have lost some of your old friends," says he, " and your reception may not be brilliant—that does not matter—say what you are doing in India, and what you mean to do. People will listen, will think about it, and after a time, you will see that the seeds will spring up." Nearly as cordial has been the reception by Mr. Rhys Davids, the great Buddhistic scholar. Long and enthusiastically did he talk of Hinduism and Buddhism, and offered to help the Indian cause to the best of his power. I have no doubt of the signal utility of his kind service. My countrymen and fellow theists will see that we have nothing to complain of in the reception given to their representative and servant. Last Sunday I preached at the Bermondsey Town Hall, where I got a congregation of 2,000 men and women. All my future Sundays in May are already engaged. Work is multiplying around me. Misrepresentations are being speedily removed. I am equally friendly, and mean to be so to all parties. With each one the New Dispensation has some bond of union. It is only those who secretly bear ill-feeling to the good cause that will keep aloof. I can only be sorry for them and supplicate Heaven for their return, I have no compromise to make, no one to conciliate. Party feelings run high in this country. In them I have neither part nor lot. I only claim to be heard. And then I feel assured Truth shall prevail.' I shall from time to time tell my friends how I am progressing. Let them give me the grace of their affection and good will. Let them pray for me, and my lonely home. Bless my work in the spirit of the Lord. Let them count me as one of them, as one of their servants.

And with God's help I will accomplish my pilgrimage, and keep our common faith before mankind.

The City of London.

To describe London would be to count the waves of the sea. It is an oft-repeated, vain, useless undertaking. The best I can do is to say how I feel—walking, weary, footsore, or perched on the top of the leviathan omnibus, I can but groan out my experiences. This perpetual peripatetic restlessness is the opposite of all true Aryan repose. These calls, balls, breakfasts, at homes, and garden parties are not the right path to Nirvana. Mr. Rhys Davids of Brick Court, Temple, told me that the 80 ton guns were all the offspring of Tamas, and so were absentee landlords, but I think he could include many things more. Nay I behold humanity no longer in items, but in grand totals. Oh! the swirling, jumping, bellowing, whistling population of the London streets—the crashing, roaring, rumbling traffic. If the vocations, resolutions, desires, disappointments, pursuits, joys, miseries, sins and virtues of these eddying, ill-dressed, well-dressed, greasy and scented masses of men and women could be recorded, how many Babels will that make ? If the contents of these shops, cellars, garrets, godowns, houses, carts, vehicles, and newspapers were recorded, what a universe of created vanities will that make. It is bewildering to observe all this —I am but an atom in the infinite man. Yet how well-kept, well-rounded, self-conscious, self-concentrated every atom is ! A man's only protection against the insanity of centrifugal forces lies here. Another Parsee youth has blown up his brains! London is the pandemonium of unbalanced boys who come to England in scores. It gives the most ample training for madness and eccentricity. Infuse power and purpose into Hindu youths, give them centre, guidance, recommend them to public opinion when you bid them come here. Or the elaborate machinery of civilization will crush all life, character, and manhood out of them. Wine and woman sit at the gates of that civilization, and many are the victims they take.

MAY MEETINGS.

As the bloom comes to the hawthorn, and the

green leaf to the vine and chesnut, so intellectual and sentimental fervor to John Bull's capacious "liver" in the month of May. He winds up his twelve months' work and benevolence by speechifying at Exeter Hall. The enthusiasm is at its white heat, and many a reputation is made or marred in May. The meetings are either religious or social. The former are mostly orthodox, the latter mostly Temperance. Returning from those missionary and propagation of gospel meetings, it is impossible to conclude that Christian faith is waning. Millions of gold are freely spent for the conversion of the heathen, and the spread of Christian literature. The orthodox speeches are not very fine, but the orthodox practices are glorious. May their efforts never grow less. The social meetings are no less characteristic. The cause of Temperance has perceptibly advanced during the last ten years. Not only have local option and Sunday closing bills made considerable progress in Parliament, but the people have come to be convinced of the evil of drinking. Fine temperance hotels have sprung up both in London, and the provinces. A larger number of ministers, both churchmen and non-conformists, have zealously enlisted themselves as Temperance reformers. Publicans and brewers are distinctly gaining in unpopularity, and coffee-houses are multiplying everywhere. I find the anti-opium agitation is also becoming strong. Though the revenue difficulty of the Indian Government meets with extensive sympathy, to me there seems to be every likelihood of the disgust against opium traffic growing stronger and stronger. Great changes are in store for India. The mill-owners' memorial against the present practice of liquor licencing in Bengal has created surprise and indignation in every one who has seen it. The recklessness of Government policy in liquor traffic you may rest assured, is now doomed.

THE ANGLO-INDIAN AT HOME.

With a blazing cheerful fire by his side, long packets of paper before him, paler and thinner than he ever was in India, sits the Earl of Northbrook in his official residence at the Admiralty. He is thoughtful, inquisitive, kind-hearted, and just. His presence is a consolation and encouragement to every Indian who has the privilege to see him. His interest in great questions is unabated, and he is the natural guide of the Indian policy of Her Majesty's Government. Speaking of the agitation on the Criminal Procedure Amendment Bill he said "My excellent countrymen in India are sometimes stark mad, I am sorry to say." And then he examined the nature of the small measure that is before the Council. The conversation left but little doubt that Mr. Ilbert's bill would pass. Only the application of the principle and privileges of the Bill would be very limited at first. The conservatives you know have made a great party question of it, and that model orator, Lord George Hamilton, wise as he is young, is trying to act the role of a London Branson.

Sir Arthur Hobhouse is as busy as ever, and Lady Hobhouse as serene and motherly as before. Their home at Bruton Road is the resort of many Anglo-Indians, and some distinguished Hindus. They are both in sound health, their Indian sympathies matured by the action of a noble and vigorous English atmosphere of thought. It was in their house you meet with Sir George Campbell, like an aged kite, whose youth has ceased to be renovated. Whitening, hobbling, uttering feeble sentences, the fallen hero picks his way through the room. But he is a staunch Liberal for all that, speaking in and out of season. It is there you meet with Sir Richard Temple with his Star of India round his neck. It is there you meet with Rajah Rampal Sing, busy with English and Indian politics, and desirous of inviting every body to dinner.

INDIA OFFICE.

But if you wish to contemplate the great variety of Anglo-Indian officials, you cannot do better than perambulate the India office. There the atmosphere is calm, and silence reigns. The laced and lettered messengers flit out and in ; the helmeted policeman as sentry is black and solemn; thoughtful owls, and massive dancing girls darkened with smoke, are carved out of the stone cornice. It is a place where the whole world might well go to sleep. You behold Sir William Muir, bright and tall, sitting at his table leisurely and reciting Hindi proverbs. Sir Barrow Ellis is nursing his gout and making himself useful in the Northbrook Club, which I don't think will come to much good. The small young Indians will find it too big a place to find themselves in element. It is destined, I am afraid, to remain as a respectable anachronism, well-endowed, well-inaugurated, but without practical interest to any one. Sir. Bartle Frere lives at Wimbledon, a suburban paradise where cabmen are insolent, roads are steep, and dust is plentiful. Lady Frere does the hospitality, abuses the Government, and Sir Bartle taciturn, only consenting to show himself The Anglo-Indian is not uncompanionable in London by any means. There are great shiploads of them coming. They have created some opinion on the Ilbert Bill. One hears a good deal of Mr. Norris, your Judge, from Unitarians both of Bristol and London. He is liked by few who know him best. But they say the attack on him in the *Bengalee* was injudicious. Mr. Norris, before he leaves India, will make himself yet *felt*.

JOHN BRIGHT AT BREAKFAST.

John Bright eats his breakfast like a lion, and digests it too. But he does not drink. He is a broad middle-sized man with great soft hands, and an enormous appetite. I have seen him finish off the plentiful morning meal with half a jug of milk and a good lump of solid sugar. which he puts into his mouth somewhat surreptitiously. John calls out for cigars when the rest of the eating is done. He produces from his well worn pouch different sizes, and if any of his companions is conscientious about smoking, presents him with a small and mild Havanna. He sat at table the observed of all observers. They asked him all manner of questions, and at last the subject of Indian administration turned up. There is no man fit to govern India at the present moment, said he except perhaps Gladstone; but we cannot expect more than one Gladstone in a century, and he has plenty to do at home. He was asked what sort of Government he would propose for India. He said he would desire the abolition of the post of Governor

General who, chiefly confined to Bengal, did not see enough of the country. Difficulties often arose between the Viceroy and the provincial Governors, whose local experience often gave them an advantage over him. Difficulties also often arose between Her Majesty's minister at home and the Governor General, who, if he was a man of ability and honesty, did not quietly submit to the dictation of the India office. Again in the case of an ambitious man like Lord Dalhousie, or an incompetent man like Lord Lytton, the whole country was precipitated into complications and hostilities which men with smaller jurisdiction might not incur. He would therefore break up the present Government of India into smaller Governorships with direct relations to the Government at home, each with its provincial army, and powers over taxation and revenue. It is impossible, he said, to expect that the Indian population could ever form one nation. It is absurd to think that 250 millions of men and women can consider themselves one people. So the best way of connecting them together would be to help them to form a number of small distinct nationalities according to their origin, antecedents, sympathies, and dialects. This unity the governments which he proposed ought to promote. India, said Mr. Bright, had been acquired by enormous crimes. The English Government can only atone for them by teaching the people how to govern themselves. For in the course of time, near or remote, England shall have to leave India to itself, if the teachings of history be true. It may perhaps not be the Indians who will compel her to do so, the affairs of Europe will some day compel her to do so. It is not in the nature of things that 50 millions of men can hold 250 million for ever. When England leaves, if one may venture to indulge in a little prophecy, the people of India will first quarrel, the powerful among them trying to conquer the less powerful, and then they will settle down not into one government, nor into one nationality, but different small organizations of Government. He proposed to anticipate that contingency, by providing for it in the plan thus laid out by himself.

The conversation then turned upon the present agitation in India. I hope, said Mr. Bright, that

Lord Ripon will serve out his full term, get the bill passed, and then return home. I have known Lord Ripon since he was a child, he has ever been faithfully attached to the Liberal interests. His conversion into Roman Catholicism for a time cast some darkness over his name. But they did not know the causes, and therefore blamed him. He had few relatives of his own, and his wife's brothers and sisters were like his own relatives. The tragical death of Mr. Vining at the hand of Greek bandits exercised a strange effect on his mind, and led him to take a different view of human life. No one has ever dared to doubt his earnestness or sincerity. Little before he started for India I met Lord Ripon one day at Piccadilly going towards Kensington, and asked him about his appointment. "Rest assured'' said Lord Ripon "any change in my religious belief has made no change in political principles. I have been offered by Mr. Gladstone this great appointment, and I will try to discharge its duties faithfully." Mr. Bright expressed the highest confidence in the character and principles of Lord Ripon. He spoke, I am sorry to say, most contemptuously of the East Indians and Europeans who have joined the agitation. "Do they not know," he asked "that all Englishmen strongly dislike them ? What do they hope to gain from identifying themselves against men with whom they hold every interest in common ?" I could not answer this question. He then came to speak of a great many Indian gentlemen whom he personally knew, and among others of Mr. Lalmohun Ghose. He said, the people of India had in later times gained a good deal of political power. He laid great stress on the liberty of press. The conversation just for a moment turned on the *Bengalee* contempt of court case. Mr. Bright's opinion of Sir Richard Garth's abilities is any thing but complimentary. But Mr. Bright said the editor of the *Bengalee* had done a foolish thing, only he had suffered more for it than he ever deserved.

On being asked whether India could ever hope to gain the right of electing her representatives for the British Parliament, he said "that was not possible, for the simple reason that you would absolutely swamp us with your votes." But he said an Indian could very well represent an English constituency if it would have him. This was very largely a question of expense. He had been once or twice spoken to on this subject by Indian gentlemen in England. But after these men went back to their Native country he never heard from them again. He said there still rang in his mind a simple sentence which had been uttered by a Hindu who had come to see him. "No one ever cared for my poor country!" Mr. Bright spoke with touching admiration of Sir Salar Jung, and fully dwelt upon the espionage and ill-treatment under which he had to drag the latter part of his life. There is quite one opinion on this subject, and the restoration of the Berars in England. They are all waiting to see what is next going to be done in the Nizam's Government. Mr. Bright sets his face against violent agitation of every kind. He said, "Never be persuaded to use violence either in speech or act. Every reform has to be won constitutionally, inch by inch, in this country. Be not tired to try to obtain your rights. You have already obtained some, you shall have more. But never be violent in anything. All progress has its laws, and act slowly. If you do not get all you want, your children will. What our fathers did not have, we have. The future must be allowed to mend the past."

Thus the breakfast was to us a feast of ideas and flow of soul. The remnants of food were removed. The cigars were finished, the ashes grew cold on the saucers, we all got up. And as I was going to leave, Mr. Bright asked me how the missionaries of the Brahmo Somaj found their living. When he heard they took no salary, and devoted their whole time and energy to the work of the church, he exclaimed, " I see, they rely upon Providence to feed them. Well there is a great deal in that. It is not every one that can rely upon Providence, but those that can need look up to no other support." The conservatives in the House of Commons under Sir Stafford Northcote charged Mr. Bright with a sort of libel, otherwise called "breach of privilege." But they had to withdraw their charge, and the motion was thrown out by a majority of votes.

Such is John Bright, the people's tribune. He is the type of the true Englishman, firm, bold, truthful, and profoundly religious. His honor and affection for Mr. Gladstone are great, and there is no doubt these feelings are reciprocated. They make England what she now is. And long may John Bright live and work for the benefit of his countrymen and the welfare of mankind.

AN ENGLISH POLITICAL FESTIVAL.

The wealthy borough of Birmingham is celebrating a great festival. It is the twenty-fifth year of the political relationship between John Bright and that town. For full quarter of a century now have the interests of the voters of Birmingham been represented in Parliament by Mr. Bright. And during the past week the great population, led by their Mayor and Town Council, have expressed their sense of his services. It is a tremendous occasion. It gives us an adequate insight into the political soul of a great English community. And as we all are just acquiring a little national vitality in that line, it will not be unprofitable to describe some of the doings which I have seen. It may be worth while to begin by saying that John Bright did not himself seek the honor of election by Birmingham. But the constituency sought him and made him their representative in 1858. In his absence, in his temporary retirement from public life, they elected him asking no questions, wanting no pledges. During these twenty-five years the constituency of Birmingham has multiplied tenfold in electoral franchise, and the poor have a voice with the rich in the management of their own affairs. That voice has made itself heard during the last week. The name of the present festival is John Bright Celebration. It commenced on Monday last, the 11th June. The population turned out to receive Mr. Bright at the railway station, and escort him through the town to a suburban park called Aston. The flags were few and far between, and the scanty bunting, here and there hung across the streets, looked more like the household wash spread out in the sun than any festive drapery. The helmeted policeman was more ornamental than useful, but the people were gathering fast. About noon every balcony bore its load of well-dressed women, every window its mass of crowded holiday makers, and every street corner its surging sea of heads. The slanting slated roofs held in their perilous cornices groups of squatting half-reclined humanity, and even the lampposts and chimney tops were manned. John Bright medals had been struck in silver, bronze, and lead. John Bright photographs were selling for a penny. John Bright ribbons adorned every breast. The news-boys were every second hawking about the programme. The wheeled coffee machine was doling out refreshments, ice creams and "hoky poky" were selling very cheap. The ill-dressed street-crowds were exchanging jests and compliments. At about two in the afternoon the mounted police in the far distance began to rear their horses, the corners and roadways were spaced out, the roaring crowd swayed backwards and forwards, and the distant notes of bands of music came floating in the air. The great cavalcade with John Bright was approaching. Spectacles were planted deeper on the nose, parasols were tossed back, binoculars were raised, a great hum, like a tidal wave, emerged, the procession was near! Far away the banners glimmered in the bright sun; on the polished metal of the harness of the splendid horses the daylight flashed, flashed on the helmets of the gallant fire brigade; hundreds of vehicles, horsesmen, bands of music, and political bodies came marching bravely at the van. The oranges were laid aside half-eaten on the window ledge, the newspapers were laid aside half-read, the biscuits dropped unheeded from hands and pockets, the pipe was as good as not smoked at all. The excitement was at a white heat. Banner came after banner square, oblong, and triangular, some large enough to screen the road, held by great posts resting on men's girdles and breast pouches, some on horseback, and some carried in hand. Each banner was borne by a trade or by a political association, the members of which either marched on foot hand to hand, or rode in elegant carriages drawn by one, two, and four horses. The braziers marched behind a giant-looking man in a glittering brass armour, encasing him from head-to foot in feudal fashion. The bakers marched with portentous loaves, and rolls of bread of preternatural size in cars. There were the silversmiths, electro-platers, button-makers, and manufacturers of hardware. Each of these trading communities bore enthusastic testimony by voice, band, and inscription to the free commercial principles for which Mr. Bright had fought. But the bakers were most demonstrative, and their symbols were in commemoration of the Anti-corn Law agitation. But none could compete in zeal and warmth with the thousands of working men whom Mr. Bright had provided with more plentiful bread, with higher wages, with decent homes, and political suffrage. The demonstration was that of the people, that of the poor, of the grateful myriads of the masses. It was a wonderful spectacle to behold how these sturdy free born men paid the homage of their hearts to a great national leader. It was an affecting sight to observe how sincere, well-tried, long, unselfish services at last forced their due tribute in a profusion of honor which was almost adoration and idolatory. Mr. Bright's picture was carried in a kind of metal shrine, laced, flowered, festooned most elaborately, reminding one very much of Hindu deities, and the Roman Catholic Madonna. Showers of small bits of paper flew from the window serving both for response, and advertisement! The Mayor rode in his state-carriage and four, the aldermen were heavily fettered with official gold-chains, the crowds hurraed, and last of all came the open carriage of John Bright himself. The abundant masses of silver hair fell on his sides, and mixed with the ample whiskers of equal whiteness. The large, full, powerful face was florid, almost red, dignified, imperturbable, perhaps sad. Was he realizing the vanity of human situations? One day so unpopular, so well-abused, feared, shunned, nearly deposed; and to-day borne as it were on a cloud of glory, with honor ahead, and gratitude behind. One day branded almost as a traitor, his friends distrustful, his party wavering, his foes exultant. To-day riding home like a Roman victor, amidst universal acclaim, his friends in triumph, his principles recognized, his foes even joining in the homage of praise and love. Thus the procession passed on, thus the day was spent. When the evening approached the great population moved in the direction of Aston where the fire-works were to be. Popular games were going on. The swings revolved by steam power. The merry gorounds were worked by engines. And among other contrivances there were strange receptacles like ships, with sails full-spread, which went up and down the air like vessels at sea, tossing, pitching, lurching from side to side, giving the riders all the agreeable sensations of real sea-sicknesses. Carriages, carts, omnibuses, were being piled along the roads. The fire-works were to begin at nine o'clock. Amidst all these arrangements one singular feature was the absence of drunkenness. Temperance has made wonderful progress in England. And there is a consequent absence of violence. The police had very little indeed to do. The people by good humour and mutual forbearance managed every thing. John Bright is the champion of peace and temperance. But he has some weakness for oranges and cigars. In the open carriage while riding amdist the procession, he had behind his head two bright red oranges. I did not see him suck them, but I have no doubt they were now and then attacked. In the great Bingley Hall assembly, where twenty-two thousand men congregated to hear him on Wednesday the 13th, you could see an orange blooming amidst the state papers. And it is a notorious fact that John Bright cannot digest his breakfast of boiled salmon which he fishes with his own hands, without a helpful cigar. That Bingley Hall meeting was a tremendous affair. The assembly of twenty thousand sang the people's anthem, "Auld Lang Syne," and "Johny comes marching home again," with a gusto which must be heard. While the one hundred and fifty addresses were being read, the bodies of delegates were filing past the hero's chair, the applause and cheers rang, and roared like thunder, great John blushed red like a girl of nineteen. The favorite orange was forgotten, the papers in his well-worn hat stood neglected. He shut his eyes, he passed his hands nervously over his heated brows, evidently his confusion was great. And when the time came for him to get up and speak, and the crowds burst out in a tremendous outcry of applause, for a moment the "people's tribune" stood dumb-foundered, then he stoutly went on thus :—"How shall I speak to this vast assembly? How shall I answer the more than 150 addresses which have been presented to me? How shall I thank my friends for their profuse and costly gifts? How shall I find words to express the thoughts with which my heart is filled? I can only bid you to imagine the thoughts of gratitude, which it is not possible to put into words, for the extraordinary manifestations of regard and friendship with which you have favoured me. But still there comes the question again— How shall I speak to this vast assembly?" But he spoke nevertheless. Spoke as he alone can speak. And the scene that night will be remembered in Birmingham for decades. It is not the pomp and display, the military brilliance or the flags and symbols of this festival that are noteworthy. It is the enthusiasm, the loyalty, the gratitude of the people that give it an unprecedented significance. And the expressions of such feelings

Make the pagentries of Kings like shadows seem.
And unsubstantial dreams.

THE ATLANTIC.

No visit to America can be described without a few words about the Atlantic. That is a dreaded ocean. To me it showed all its fierceness. From the 15th of August when I left Liverpool almost continuously to the 21st, a regular gale blew from the North-West. There was occasional rain, the darkness was fearful with a tremendous sea. On Sunday the 19th it grew into a regular storm. The waves were heaving mountains high, they broke round the ship with a thundering crash. The poor old vessel, about which more by and bye, pitched and lurched, swayed and struggled, shivering every moment from stem to stern, from keel to mast. The wind was an indescribable howl of fury, and the black, hollowing, mad waters beat a fitting response. The tattered, rushing, deepening clouds seemed to come lower and lower. Blinding masses of heavy salt spray rose out of the waves, and drenched everything. Great volumes of water came bounding and splashing over the sides, and over the head of the vessel. The cabins were swamped, books, slippers, boxes swimming about. The decks were overflowing, streams rolled in every direction with the tottertng ship. The tables were deserted; the plates, glasses, knives and dishes knocked about as if some demon was let loose amongst them. The ship carried about 400 emigrants or steerage passengers. These belonged to the poorest of all European countries, chiefly Ireland. Men, women, priests, babies, boys, editors, roughs, wags, poets, labourers of every description. Every one was vomitting, or about to vomit, crouching, reclining unsafe on rickety deck chairs, or holding by the rails. Strange looking people who lie down together in heaps in every imaginable corner, squat, spit, smoke, laugh, jabber, fiddle, pipe, or dance, and on the whole behave good humouredly in this stress of weather. The captain had to abandon the Sunday service. There was an Anglican clergyman on board, but he lay on his back gasping with sea sickness behind the funnel. I alone sat mute and shivering in the cold rain and wind, on the top deck. I watched those grand billows, as they formed, rose, crested themselves with foam, gleamed for a moment with their great blue necks, like some supernatural serpents, and then broke round the ship in instant thunder. To the utmost verge of the horizon nothing was perceptible, but cloud, rain, wretchedness, wind, roar, and approaching terror.

But if the Atlantic is fearful in a storm, there is no glory greater than the glory of that ocean in fair weather. To me this was all the more joyous for the trouble experienced over the greater part of the voyage. The last few days of the passage were exceedingly bright. Bright weather is a marvel of nature in this sea. There is sunshine all over the world, but here sunshine calls out the profoundest life out of everything. Every color, even the flaring rags hung about as the ship's bunting, suggest wonderful secrets. In this many-hued joyousness, infancy, youth, manhood, and strange experiences of all sorts lie blended. There is blue all over the world. But this resplendent rippling blue, bluer than all heaven and earth, relieves the sight and responds to it, speaking in half articulate sounds to the universe, and to the mind. Every one ought to see the Atlantic sunset, the sadness of the great sight when the softened sweetened orb sinks into the far waters of West. As if the glory from from some living all-influencing soul is slowly passing away. But the heaven glows and the ocean flames after the sun's departure. And then the mild stars come out one by one. And new light dawns upon the world like the Pentecostal spirit. Gaze into those great star depths. They are all above the so called sky. The infinite beyond is peopled with lustrous masses of universe, deep within deep, high above high. Like the sounds of the sea, creations abound and crowd everywhere. The magic of the Atlantic light and darkness dissolves every thing.

On the 28th of August, after a tedious voyage of 13 days I arrived at Boston. The very first thing about America that strikes the stranger is the fineness of outlook. The coal grime smoke, cloud, wet and unnamable blackness of old England are left behind the briny Atlantic. It is a bright land, the land of the setting sun.

The air is crisp, and pours vitality into you. The harbour of Boston is in itself an inspiration. It is studded with little wooded islands; a hospital here, a fort there, a penitentiary, or a pleasure house. It looks like a sea, with the caves and grottos of mirmaids and water nymphs. It is Grasmere, or Loch Lomond expanded, it is an illimitable Rhine with Rhenish haunts on a large scale. The steamers, yachts, and tenders have a white-washed smart look. The buildings, and flagstaffs seem to be in a sort of honey, moon. After the sombre hues of Orthodox Europe the western hemesphere makes one cry out " hail holy light." This effect might have been heightened in me by the rough voyage.

One hears of the fabulous grandeur of the Cunard steamers, they are compared to floating hotels, to sailing palaces, to oceanic cities and what not. As a set off to all this imperial magnificience the company run at intervals some of their old cast away boats which in their dirt and discomfort rival the Arab Dhow, or the Spanish slave galley. It was my lot to select one of these rare ships. It is said this will be about the last trip which the "Marathon" makes across the Atlantic, and that henceforth she will be relegated to the Mediterranean traffic, as the lame horse from a gentleman's stables is consigned to the Cab. I hope that for the peace of future tourists this may be so. But if the vessel was a failure, the officers on board were the patterns of good humour and attention.

THE PEOPLE OF AMERICA.

The first impression I got of the Yankee differentiated him sufficiently from the people of the old world. When the government surgeon at Boston harbour stepped over from the pilot brig into the "Marathon" to examine our bill of health, I scanned him narrowly. I afterwards found nearly the whole of the United States presented a repetition of this main type of face and features. A closely cropped head, almost clean shaven, with a thin whitish down overspreading the crown, a pale well-knit countenance, the lank limbs surmounted by a broad-brimmed, black-ribboned straw hat, with a strip of chipped wood stuck into the mouth, complete the outfit of Brother Jonathan. He wears thin woollen clothing, does not burden himself with an over-coat, and is not fond of a beard ; he often chews tobacco, and has the quality of spitting most energetically, incessantly, and scientifically straight. Yet it is a fact there is more abstinence from wine and tobacco in America than in any country in Europe. From his personal appearance however you ought to be able to tell an American from an Englishman.

The American from the Northern States will perhaps vary from the Southerner in the fact that the latter shows a little more of Continental Europe in his face and manners. The American from the North has more of the English and Scotch in him. The American of the South has more of the Spaniard, Italian, and German in him. He will sometimes cultivate a heavy patch of hair on his underlip, coming down the chin stiff and square like a clothes-brush. He will carry a revolver in his pocket, smoke and chew, show a quickness of temper, and a universal contempt for men and things in general. The Western Yankee or cowboy as he is called, is more primitive than either, with the traditional Nankeen trowsers, dirty top-boots, long bowie knife, and six-chambered pistol stuck in his belt. He talks loudly, drinks incessantly, spits recklessly, bullies every body, and "guesses" without intermission.

The emancipated Negro is a large, pompous, white-waist-coated individual, 270 averaging lbs in weight. He has a wide good-humoured grin, wears false gold chains, and makes excellent waiters at the hotels. His weakness is for spring chicken and roast pig, with a drop too much of whiskey. He fills the situation of porter at the Pulman car, can do himself credit as a coach-man, smacking his whip with a white-gloved hand, to the admiration of bystanders. The Negro is an important politician, voting for the republican ticket, and is as good as any other man in getting up a row on election day. The Negro likes to attend school, and a good many pathetic tales are told as to how he managed to pick up a little book knowledge in the days of slavery. In those times it was criminal to teach a Negro to read and write. And it is said——"One negro who served in a private family contrived to pick up his letters in this way: He had been sent one day to do somthing to the stove in the room where the governess was teaching the children. He did his work as quietly as possible, listening to the governess, watching stealthily the letters to which she pointed, and trying to fix in his memory the names she gave them. He made his work at the stove last as long as possible, and went away with half the alphabet in his memory. After that, when cleaning the room in the morning, he would examine these letters carefully, and go over their names. But how to get the names of the rest!—that was now his difficulty. One morning the little boy, a son of the proprietor, came into the room. The two were alone, and Sam thought, "Now is my chance."

"You' se mighty smart wid your lessons, I hears, Massa Tom," he said.

Master Tom assented promptly.

"Reckon you know a mighty heap of dem tings on de wall dere. But you dunno," he said experimentally, "what dem black tings is," and pointed to the alphabet.

"I do. I know every one of them."

"Come now, you dunno what dey call dis chap, standin' wid his legs in de air?"

"Yes. I do. That's Y."

"Wye! Lor'whot a name to gib him! But you dunno de name of dis yer one sittin' on de ground!"

"Yes, I do. That's I."

"Lor! Why, Massa Tom, you knows eberyting. Reckon you know dat one too,"—pointing to another; and so he went on till he had got the names of all the letters he had previously missed. This man, before the war came to set him free, had learned to read and write with tolerable ease."

I was present in Washington at a great Colored public meeting. About two thousand people were present. A Colored orator whose name I forget just now, made a very long violent speech against the tyranny of the whites. The occasion was most interesting. When I speak of the Colored population it must not be imagined they are all black. Some of them are so white, and so positively beautiful, the women specially, that no unpractised eye like mine, can note the least difference between them and the whites. Yet the slightest tinge of African blood in such people causes their enumeration among the blacks. Lightness of complexion in mixed descent constitutes no advantage in this country as in India. The white half-caste can not look down upon the darker skin as his inferior. To the impartial American they are all equal. No social intercourse of any kind is possible with the Colored man. He will not be admitted into the first class hotel. He cannat travel in the Pulman palace car. He can not send his children for education into the great colleges of the country. In the North the distinctions are perhaps less sharply observed, but in the South they are insurmountable. Yet it is a singular fact that in all the audiences I have addressed, numbering sometimes thousands, I did not observe at any time a single Negro who came to hear me. So strong is caste in America still.

THE VASTNESS OF AMERICA.

My whole nature is impressed with the greatness of the American continent and people. It holds in itself the hopes and promise of the world's future. England excels in the richness of her political and intellectual life. America excels in her boundless vitality of every kind. England has formulated her physical and mental resources in institutions, usages, churches, and organizations; they are vigorous, mature, almost perfect. America has quite as many or more organizations, and has still a universe of surplus energy left, full of perpetual scheming. England is a small island, America is a vast continent. England is one nation only, America is the conglomorate of all European nationalities with quite a considerable infusion of Africa and China. The pouring emigration into America amounts to about 300,000 souls a year. English cities are populous and old. In a few years a new city springs up in the American wilderness containing hundreds of thousands of inhabitants. Take Chicago on the lake Michigan. A little over forty years ago it was nonexistent, and the wild aborigines roamed over the lake-side. So late as 1830 Chicago was a small government outpost with four taverns, one merchant, one butcher, and no clergyman at all. Today Chicago has a population of 600,000 which she promises to double in the course of a decade! Cities are multiplying in the western and southern parts of the United States with marvellous speed, and inhabitants from every corner of the globe are streaming into them. New York is absorbing its neighbouring islands, and extending its arms across the rivers and creeks. Brooklyn, one of the suburbs, has a population of more than 300,000 souls! The whole land seems to be replete with a gigantic Titanic life. The industry is immense, the wealth is immense, the life is inexhaustible. In half a century more America will cast its shadow over the whole habitable globe. A single gold mining company in California annually produces 37 million dollars worth of the precious metal. The grains, the fruits, the meats of America travel to the ends of the earth. Every thing goes forward at a prodigious rate. Education is free, and reaches the lowest strata of the population. The prospects of men in every sphere of life are unbounded. A squatter or back woodsman may any day accumulate his millions, go to New York, and control the elections. The son of a man who lives in the log-shanty to-day, may, thirty years hence, become the President of the Republic. The Union Pacific Railroad extends over nearly four thousand miles from East to West. The lakes are great inland seas. You can sail one thousand to fifteen hundred miles up and down the great rivers. The wild uninhabited prairies are thousands of square miles in extent. And all this is one country, under one government, speaking one language, having mainly the same feelings and aspirations. The characteristic of the population is its sense of youth, and determination to go forward in everything. Religion, politics, literature, science, social reform, mercantile speculation, wealth, luxury, infidelity, eccentricity, everything has its charm and novelty in America. The Irish are there, the Germans are there, the Swedes and Italians are there, the Negroes and Chinese are there, the American Indians, and shades, grades, and half-castes of every denomination are there, seething in one vast cauldron of humanity. The Roman Catholics are flourishing greatly; the organizations and churches to disseminate agnosticism and atheism are prospering as well. Monsigneur Cappel is lionized, Matthew Arnold is worshipped, and they burn incense to Herbert Spencer. In Newport, Rhode Island, which is the Brighton of America, the rage is to imitate every English fancy and folly, and the American swells have taken to fox-hunting much to the disgust of staid old fashioned Yankeeism. And in New York, O'Donovan Rosa, with his colleagues are fulminating their fenianism, and arranging programmes of dynamite and destruction. The purists of Philadephia are influencing the government and the nation for an armed intervention to put down Mormon polygamy on American soil; while the elders of Salt Lake City are shipping thousands of pilgrims from the chief European ports to swell the inmates of their happy homes. Three car loads of prospective wives and pluralistic husbands had arrived the night before I was in Utah. All the extravagances of a new, youthful, redundant national vitality are in America. The raw meterials, and unripe energies will take time to tone and settle down. What the future will be, it is difficult to tell. The uncontrolled forces of the present will by and bye indicate their normal direction. Many troubles are likely to come before that takes place however. Yet there is a wonderful measure of regularity in things even now. America shows the phases of a mighty evolution of humanity.

AMERICAN FREEDOM.

Freedom is of course the watch-word of American society. Democracy has assimilated itself with the vitals of every man and woman. You notice it in unexpected quarters. The hotel porter accosts you most familiarly, and demands to know your business in America. The chamber-maid bids you wait till she can find time to "fix up" your room. The railway, or street car conductor cordially takes his seat very close to you, and spits away once every second almost, while he puts away his democratic feet at right angles with your face. All classes, communities, and sexes are herded together in the same vehicles to accomodate each other as best as they can. The newspapers like police detectives, search out every man's personal history, private proclivities and domestic arrangements, praising, patronizing, abusing, exposing, cutting up as American newspapers only can. Their reporters respect neither persons, nor privacies, consult neither health, nor convenience, but interview every one, ask every question, and do not scruple to make the minutest inquiries. If you decline to answer these the most outrageous descriptions of your personal appearance, your views and principles, probably come out in the next day's paper. Strange and dreadful charges of bribery and corruption are preferred against public officers, who retort by running down their critics as mercilessly. A great drawback to freedom is the enormous demand for money created by a highly artificial society, imaginary wants, and fastidious tastes which have now become second nature with the people. So men and women in every sphere of life have to work at a high pressure, most detrimental to health and comfort. The pallor on the face, the premature grayness of the hair, the careworn anxious looks, the incessant persistent activity everywhere, in every one, even children not excepted, tell of the tremendous necessity for money making which actuates the nation. There is a new disease universally spoken of in America. It is "nervous prostration." And there are "nervine hospitals" in all the important towns which receive and reco-operate the worked out members of society. Nervous collapse is the sure result of the slavish search for worldly aggrandizement. Amusements, comforts, the demands of family and of society are sacrificed at the stern altar of "business." With the best of intentions men cannot find time to what they wish as citizens, as friends, as members of society. Business swallows personal freedom. The possession of wealth becomes the passport to influence, position, honour. And men madly rush after that. "Ill fares the land," the poet says, "to hastening ills a prey, where wealth accumulates, and men decay."

"What I have seen and heard during my stay among you," says Herbert Spencer, "has forced on me the belief that this slow change from habitual inertness to persistent activity has reached an extreme from which there must begin a counterchange and reaction. Everywhere I have been struck with the number of faces which told in strong lines of the burdens that had to be borne. I have been struck too with the large proportion of gray-haired men, and enquiries have brought out the fact that with you the hair commonly begins to turn some ten years earlier than with us. Moreover in every circle I have met with men who had themselves suffered from nervous collapse due to stress of business, or named friends who had either killed themselves by overwork, or had been permanently incapacitated, or had wasted long periods in endeavours to recover health. I do but echo the opinion of all observant persons I have spoken to that immense injury is being done by this high pressure of life."

"You retain, the forms of freedom, but so far as I can gather, there has been a considerable loss of the substance. It is true that those who rule you do not do it by means of retainers armed with swords, but they do it through regiments of men armed with voting papers, who obey the word of command as loyally as did the dependants of the old feudal nobles, and who thus enable their leaders to override the general will, and make the community submit to their exactions as effectually as their prototypes of old. It is doubtless true that each of your citizens votes for the candidate he chooses for this or that office, from president downward, but his hand is guided by an agency behind, which scarcely leaves him any choice. " Use your political power as we tell you, or else throw it away " is the alternative offered to the citizen. The political machinary as it is now worked, has little resemblance to that contemplated at the outset of your polifical life. Manifestly those who framed your constitution never dreamed that twenty thousand citizens would go to the poll led by a "boss," yet the fact remains that in America every body does very much what he likes. Individuals and corporations feel equally unfettered in their conduct. Conflicting rights are adjusted by outlays of money, or appeals to fire-arms. Society as well as government require further settling down. No one can form any thing more than vague and general conclusions respecting your future. The factors are too numerous, too vast, too far beyond measure in their quantities and intensities. The world has never before seen social phenomena at all comparable with those presented in the United States. A society spread over enormous tracts, while still preserving its political continuity, is a new thing. This progressive incorporation of vast bodies of emigrants of various bloods, has never occured on such a scale before. Large empires composed of different people have in previous cases been formed by conquests and annexations. Then your immense plexus of railways and telegraphs tends to consolidate this vast aggregate of States in a way that no such aggregate has ever before been consolidated. And there are many minor causes cooperating, unlike those hitherto known. No one can say how it is all going to work out." Onething however in the meantime remains certain. For the weak in body, or mind, or purse there is no chance in America. It is a regular survival of the fittest, a struggle for existence in which neither birth, nor education, neither sex nor susceptibility counts for anything. It is freedom for the strong slavery for the weak.

THE RED MAN.

It is supposed by some that the American Indian is dying out before " superior civilization." Others maintain that he is prospering and multiplying as ever. In any case the fact is undoubted that the Red man is seldom met with. In the Eastern States you don't see him at all. In the far Western regions he now and then emerges into view. He lives in the territories known as Indian Reservations. There are about 300,000 of American Indians divided into many tribes, the wildest of which are said have died out. The American Indian is a middle-sized man of disagreeable unwholesome copper complexion. He is small-eyed, flat nosed, with a ill-formed wide mouth extending from ear to ear, and straight matted tagrag hair. He generally dresses in some sort of cast-away European clothing, when he does not array himself in his native costume, which I have not seen. He has a fine brave constitution, lives chiefly by hunting and fishing, and has a nature as proud as sensitive. He remembers a kind act, and never forgets an injury. He has deep suspicion of the white man, and will never allow himself to be outwitted if he can help it. A friend of mine relates the following incident. "An American surveyor was travelling with his party in the islands of Lake Huron, and came to an Indian village. The photographer of the party set up his camera, and the natives being always very curious came in groups and stood about. As soon as he put his head under the black cloth to adjust the focus, the people shuffled about thinking it was some kind of gun, and they were going to be shot. When their chief arrived, the photographer explained his object, and allowed him to have a look at the camera under the black cloth. He was pleased, and assured his people there was no powder in the instrument. But the chief noticed that everything looked upside down in the camera, and shrewdly suspected it was the wish of the white man to take the Indians in that ridiculous posture. He secretly determined to defeat this purpose. So when the artist once more tried to range his subjects in focus, what was his surprise to find they all stood on their heads! He explained to them how the case stood, but the chief would not listen to him. And though the people were persuaded to sit on the grass, the chief insisted upon being taken with his head below, and legs up in the air, held steady by two of his subjects! These chiefs have significant names. Some of the more celebrated are "Black Foot" "Swift Antelope," "Spotted Tail." The most distinguished chief presiding over the destinies of the Sieux tribe is called "Sitting Bull." They have the previlege of riding in railway trains free of cost, but they are not allowed into the cars, and sit on the foot board, and outer platform. The Indian lives in his wigwan, with his "squaw," a hardy, fierce, industrious lady, who bears the "papoosh" the young hopeful son perched on her back. The Indians complain bitterly of the approach and aggressions of the white man. He has shot them and they have scalped him, Where ever the Indians are, robbery, fighting, and mutual extermination are going on. Some of them have been converted to Christianity, but most are not. Yet some of them are not wanting in fine sentiment and heroic inpulse. The Saes, and the Foxes, the Cherookees, Dacotas, and Sieux have some fine men among them. One of these tribes was, many years ago pushed back from province to province, and their chief had occasion to speak of the American war. He said :—

"That land was ours. But the white people began to want it for their cotton and their slaves. We said, ' No ; this is our hunting-ground. The bones of our fathers lie here. We will not part with it.' They said they must have it, one way or another. We held a council, but it broke up ; nothing could be done. Then the white people passed laws over our heads, that broke our government all to pieces. They took us prisoners for every little debt, and they made debts in order to take us prisoners. In every way they rode over us roughshod. We appealed to the Great Father at Washington. He said, 'I cannot protect you where you are. But you have lands west of the Mississippi, I will remove you there' this was what they wanted—to get us away, and take our land. We held another council. It lasted four days. I was a young man then, but I was one of the council. We said, 'This land is ours. Let us live and die here.' The Secretary of War was there, and his mouth was full of promises. But we said, 'The Secretary of War will die; the Great Father at Washington will die; and all this will be repudiated.' The Secretary had bribed one of our chiefs—a half-white and half-Indian—to sign the treaty; and soon as he got it signed he went away; the traitor also fled, for he knew that we would kill him. Order came for us now to move. We said, 'No, we have been betrayed.' Then came General Scott, with 6000 men, to drive us off at the point of the bayonet. We fought, but the white man was too strong for us. Then we said, 'We will go.' It took three years to move the nation across the Mississippi. On our way the cholera took us, and swept off our people by thousands. One of our poets and orators looked back from the Western shore of the Mississipi, and said, 'If there is a God in heaven, He will reward the Georgians and the

Mississipians for this great wrong!' And he has," continued the Indian alluding to the wreck of these States in the late war. "We did not know how it would be, but it came. God is just. He has given them the same cup to drink that they gave to us."

The fatal vice of the Red man is his craving for drink. He will sell his house and home, his gun and wigwam, desert his wife and children to obtain rum. And when he gets it he is perfectly reckless as to what becomes of him afterwards. The Americans say that the Indian is an indigestible element in their land and civilization. And it was the Indian who is said to have given to the American his name of Yankee, which is *yan ghese* in his language meaning "Long knife." The bowie knife of Brother Jonathan has thus immortalized him.

NEGRO PIETY.

The religious peculiarities of the Negro have been often noticed. He is impulsive, impressible, very excitable. This, it is sometime remarked and tends to enfeeble his character, and the Negro has never distinguished himself as a strict moralist. Whether that be so or not, it is undoubted that the great progress of Methodism in America has been kept up by widespread Negro revivals.

The ardour of their piety in the absence of intelectual culture and balance breaks forth into visions, trances, shouts, violent bodily movements. But their faith is great and touching; their sentiments are warm and tender; their effusions are joyous and enthusiastic. I do not know what headway the Salvation Army has made in the Negro community. There is great field for it there. They have perfect belief that God gives them inward experiences and revolutions. Aunt Nancy who lives in Virginia thus relates her experience :—

"One day I was hoeing in the field a little, and I was thinking some has to go to heaven, and some has to go to hell, when I hears a voice saying—'You's agoin' to hell!' And says I, 'Lord, I thinks it mighty hard I has to work and suffer while I live, and go to hell when I die." Den I heard a louder voice say, 'A few more prayers —a few more prayers, and den I'll meet yer in the way of mercy.' So that night, after I'd done work, I thought I'd go out to try and find the Lord. I went out and looked all round in the woods, and hollered as loud as I could, but I couldn't find him. Next day I went to Aunt Grace, and says I, 'Aunt Grace, I's come blind.' Aunt Grace said—'Dat's all right; pray on—a few more serus prayers.' So de next night I went out again and hollered and hollered, but I could not find Him. You see," she said, "I thought I was gwine to see Him like a nat'ral man. When I went home the cocks was crowin', and I crawled up into the loft, and fell into a trance, and in de trance I was drawed away and away, and up to a great white house, whar I knocked at the door. Well, a white lady came to the door. She had black hair, and she laughed, but she didn't make no sound in her laugh. I courtesied, and said, 'How d'y?' and she said, 'How d,y?—don't you know me?' I says, 'No.' Says she, 'You ought to know me, look at me good.' Says I, 'I thinks it's the Wirgin Mary.' 'Yes,' says she, 'come in!' Bud she took me into a large room, where there was large dresses and little dresses hanging all round the room. And she took off all the old rags I wore, and put one of them white dresses on me. And she put on a turban all covered with spangles, just like little gold dollars—you's seen um. And I had little teenty feet, and she put little slippers on um. There was a large mirror in the room; and she said, 'Now, go and see how ye like yer new dress.' While I was looking, the door opened and a white man come in. He had on black clothes, and a white vest, all covered with little gold dollars, like my turban was. And he had a ring on his head, covered with the dollars, and he had two cups in his hands. He brought them to me and said—'SALVATION and DAMNATION, which will ye have?'" The old woman, as she told this, seemed much affected, and said, with awestruck voice, "Oh, it 'pears like I can see Him now!" She continued, 'Lord,' says I, 'I'll have Salvation.' There was something white in the cup, and I drank it. It was sweet, and I tasted it in my mouth two or three days after. I left a little in the cup, and he gave it back to me and said, 'Drink all of it.' Then He said, 'My little one, now go back to de world and coax sinners to come to me.' Mind, He didn't say 'drive,' He said 'coax' 'em. Den de Wirgin told me I must take off my white dress and leave it there. I didn't want to leave it off, but she said, 'I'll keep it for ye, and if ye prove faithful, ye shall have it again.' Den I said to her, 'How's I gwine to git down?,' Says she, 'How did ye git up?' 'I come up by faith,' says I. 'Well, sez she, yer gwine down the same way. So she took hold of me and lifted me off, and I flew down just like a bird, and dere I was in de loft again."

The hynms are of a corresponding description. They are simple, and are so constructed that they can be spunk out to any length by the addition of a few words:—

"Come along, old fader, come along.
For de time it is going by,
For de angels say dere's nothin' to do
But to ring dem charming bells.
O we're almost home,
We're almost home;

We're almost home
For to ring dem charming bells."

"The next verse begins,—"Come along, old muder, come along," then "Come along, dear sister, come along;" "Come along, little chill'en," and so on, each verse only needing the alteration of one word. When the meeting was in good singing trim, I sometimes heard this continued for a considerable time, the first line being started, and the new word supplied sometimes by one person, sometimes by another. A stranger generally had a verse apportioned to him, beginning,—"Come along, dear stranger, come along;" or, "Come along, white brudder, come along," the chorus being taken up by the whole congregation and sung with great feeling."

It will be at once perceived how closely allied all this is to the Hindu Vaishnava thety. The Negroes have both the virtues and vices of the Vaishnavas. And for that reason they are very much looked down upon by the other more intellectually organized sects. The Methodists take them up, and take them up with considerable success yet the Negro is being educated.

There are schools not only for the children, but for grown up men and women also. And it is not at all an unusual spectacle to see three hundred or more Negroes and Negresses assembled, quietly learning their lessons, some of them so old as to require the aid of strong glasses to read the print of their books. There are Negro schools, Negro Colleges, and black universities now, and out of the three millions of Negro population, full one-half, it may be supposed, regularly attend instruction. It is said that intellectually the black man can never be the equal of the white man. Yet acknowledgedly the exceptions to this rule are already visible. Chief among these is Frederick Douglas of Washington. Douglas is a freed slave. He is a colossal man, with long grey crisp hair which grows horizontally about his head, and gives him the appearance of a medieval saint. He speaks faultless English, without the invariable Negro accent. In religion he is a theist, in manners and sentiments a perfect gentleman. He holds a high appointment in connection with the Washington Courts, and his sons are clerks in his office. Looking at Frederick Douglas, no one could maintain that colored men were not the intellectual equals of any men.

RELIGION.

What cynics may say of Yankee free thought, there is religion in America, intense, real religion. But like every other thing ₁American religion is free, unconventional, prosperous. Politics enter into it, largely, every social reform enters into it, the race question enters into it, trade, industry, election, newspaper management, and even popular scandals go to make a part of it. In the times of the anti-slavery agitation, the pulpit was a regular furnace of denunciation, and some preachers are said to have completely lost their wits over it. Theodore Parker wrote his sermons with loaded pistols near him. Beecher had a fugitive slave-girl in his vestry whom he called out to exhibit to his congregation. The people do not care for tame, respectable, routine piety. They demand piquancy, originality, fervor, wit, with or without much spiritual edification. When they get what they want, the congregations pay without stint or measure; they crowd to the churches. The churches are furnished in a regular style, carpeted, cushioned, warmed with hot water pipes, and ministers receive princely salaries. Mr. Beecher, I believe, receives 15000 dollars a year, and one could name a great many others who get scarcely less. The salary of a minister of tolerable standing is seldom under 5000 dollars a year. Religion means scholarship, brilliancy of speech, richness of illustration, and specimens of popular feeling. The tendency of every denomination is to liberalize its teaching within its own limits, and discard or dilute orthodoxy as much as it can. American liberalism therefore cannot be identified with any particular sect, but must be looked for in all churches alike. From this it must not be imagined that the historical or theological basis of religion is at all deficient in strength. It is to me a most hopeful sign that the absolute freedom of thought has tended to harmonize liberal religion with sound faith in the dispensations of Providence, and the sacred scriptures. In England about five millions of the public money go to maintain the integrity of the

Established Church. And if the support of the State be withdrawn from the salaries of the clergy, the so-called orthodoxy of the Anglican organization would crumble into a thousand fragments. Even as it is, with all the creeds and emoluments, "the ethics of subscription" forms an open subject of uncomplimentary criticism. In America whatever religion there is, is pure. And there is a good deal of it. Why the Roman Catholics alone number five million. There are more than two million Methodists; the Episcopalians have 2110 churches, the Baptists 17,000. It is estimated that so many as five million scholars learn in the Sunday schools. And these facts represent the religious condition of the United States alone. Placed side by side with these large figures the Unitarians cannot boast of a grand numerical following. In New York out of 460 Protestant churches, the Unitarians do not own more than three. But Boston in this respect is very different. It will not be an exaggeration to say that Boston is a Unitarian town. The University of Harvard is Unitaran in its organization and influence. And Boston and Harvard no doubt form the intellectual centre of the United States. It is unquestionable that Unitarianism has greatly influenced the theology of the country during the last half a century, and that the lines between it and Congregational churches are often difficult to trace. I am apt to think that Unitarianism has very much fulfilled its mission of liberalizing thought, and it should address itself now to cultivate spirituality and faith within its own organization. The present outlook in the theological horizon does not present much prospect in the direction of critical scholarship, for personal freethought. The utmost verge seems to have been reached on those points. The religious future of America lies undoubtedly in the hands of those who can bring back the national mind to genuine profound devotion, manly unswerving faith, and the holiness and inspiration of character. It will be expected of me to speak a word of the church of Theodore Parker. I have to say it with sincere pain. There is a small remnant of men who claim to belong to his original congregation. I am unwilling to speak much about them. Perhaps they have done all they could to perpetuate Parker's name. But alas they represent neither Parker's spirituality nor American religion. They are a very small body who simply struggle for existence. And that effort takes up their whole energy. Some of them are excellent men, and I wish they could do something to keep Parker's memory green and active. But as they are working now the inevitable will come to them, it is only a question of time. I must say Parker is universally remembered in America as the bold uncompromising theist, the doughty champion who fought for the slaves, and the degraded classes. He is said to have exposed many errors and corrected many abuses. Personally he was one of the American heroes, ranking with the bravest and best, but he was not an organizer, not a constructive genius, his religion had no principle of cohesion in it. And with his disappearance his work has dissolved. It is foolish to fight against facts. Let us thank Parker for what he did. He cleared the ground. Abiding Theism must have other basis to stand upon. The future religion of America must come from the bosom of God's Spirit. The New Light shall arise in its own time.

THE FALLS OF NIAGRA.

The very first look at these mighty waters is amazing. It seems the whole heavens have dissolved, pouring down the mountains in vast tempestuous floods that cover the horizon from end to end. The noise is infinite, the water is infinite, the scene is endless; eye can not grasp it, ear cannot measure it, the mind cannot hold its majesty. The force, the rush, the roar, the dazzle, the speed, the extent simply bewilder the imagination. The clouds of blinding spray make the grandeur more unbearable; storms of wind are generated by the breathing howling cataracts; perfect arcs of the most brilliant rainbows one has ever seen, give a strange enchantment to the scene. By some natural law the brows are calmed for contemplation, the mind is refreshed, and the whole being lifted up. Again as you approach the cataract from different points, a vague fear seizes you. The wide curling rapids, miles in breadth seemingly; the singing, sounding tearing eddies; the boundless, breathless, resistless floods roaring through ancient, upturned, weird rocks, carrying or piling up great trees and giant pines like straws; the fury and might of the descending torrents over gorge and precipice, produce an electric undefinable dread, as if there is something or some one awful behind you, as if the ground under your foot is giving way, as if the frowning precipices are about to come down, and there is neither trust nor safety in this crushing, threatening, devouring, all-encompassing force. Only a deeper assurance from within quiets the mind.

Three great inland seas, miscalled lakes, pour their boundless contents into Lake Erie. And Erie pours its waters into Ontario. The channel of communication between these last two lakes is the river Niagra, no more than about 30 miles in extent. The cataract of Niagra is the fall of this river from the mountain tops. It hardly deserves the name of river, it is "a cadence of waters" from Erie to Ontario, over gorges, precipices, in rapids, whirlpools, and sweeping torrents over an uneven mountain-locked stony bed. Erie alone is a great sheet of water 290 miles long, 65 miles wide, and 84 feet deep. When to this immense mass we add the contents of Superior, Michigan, and Huron, all three much larger than Erie itself, some idea may be formed of the measureless weight of waters that fall down at Niagra from a height 160 feet. Just above the falls, the Niagra forms itself into wide violent rapids not unlike the Ganges below Goalando in the end of July. Only the thundering roar, the whiteness of the waters under a sky that seems to become a part of the element, the dark primitive forests, the grim rocks that lie overthrown, and the wonderful islands on one of which I stood, are inconceivable to one who has not been present at the scene. The whole expanse of the heavens, the east and west, the north and south are all lighted up by the gliding, glowing, billowing surfaces of the omnipresent water. These rapids as they descend are divided by a moderately large island, called Goat Island, and hence the cataracts bifurcate before they fall. One is called the American fall, and the other is called the Horse-Shoe or Canadian Fall.

The river Niagra divides the American and Canadian shores, which are connected by a suspension bridge. There are forts on both sides. The faint whistle of a railway train is sometimes heard amidst the noise of waters. A little ferry boat plies from one coast to the other over the boiling stream, as it rushes past from the gorge yonder. The cataracts descend from a semicircular precipice of rocks which go round both the Canadian and American grounds separated, as said before by a number of most picturesque islands, of which the principal is called Goat Island. Why it is called Goat I know not, except that the Iriquois Indians who owned that part of the country at one time, tended their goats there. From the neighbouring town of Buffalo you come by rail first to the American side of the Fall. Emerging from the dingy village that skirts the depôt, the abruptness of the scene which you come to face unexpectedly astounds you. The tremendous torrent over the edge of the black precipice convinces you at once that it is a phenomenon which has its parallel nowhere. But the scene completes itself as you cross the bridge over to the Canadian shore, and approach the Horse-Shoe Falls. This is Niagra by eminence. It is an immense elemental semicircle constructed by the descending floods. The great arc will be about quarter of a mile in circumference. But the rocks, rapids, streams, seem to give many times greater magnitude to the falling waters. The millions of tons of the seething liquid poured into the unsounded caverns of the rocky cauldron below, suffer a violent rebound upwards. They jump aloft in unspeakable fury, white and foamy, a boiling concussion, a chaos of motion, force, speed, violence. The mists and vapours rise, damp, dusky, unsubstantial apparitions, the rainbows glisten, the thunders break, those perpetual thunders drown all other sound, roll for ages, having strange resemblance to the majesty of eternal silence. The breathless solitudes, without the sound of a bird, without the hum of a bee, the white expanses above and around, remind one of the spheres of untrodden snow over the Himalayas. There is a marvellous unity in the depths and designs of nature. Like unto the rush of the measureless centuries into the abyss of infinite time are those wonderful irrevocable deeps of water hurling below——like unto the endless precipitation of men, dynasties, and races into the depths of destiny, sudden and unknowable. It is like the resistless course of succeeding changes that sweep life, fortune, friendship, success, sorrow care, every thing. These endless waters admonish human meanness. You stand face to face with the tremendous world-forming all-regulating energies of Providence symbolized. Rushing, roaming, roaring for ever, before your generation, and after you are gone, these torrents intimate the wisdoms, purposes, dispensations which flow for ever. Vain frivolous thoughts be hushed, let the spirit be profound, know its own depth, and flow into the bosom of the hidden Infinite.

THE AMERICAN WOMAN.

In a land of freedom woman always enjoys light and honor. Here America is consistent.

Woman enjoys a social security, a breadth of privilege, a perfection of culture not to be met with in any other part of the world. Perhaps I must specialize here the woman of New England, but every where in America woman is free. I was invited to visit and address an institution near Boston where nearly six hundred young ladies of the best American families are educated and boarded. No girl under sixteen years is admitted into Wellesley College. And they remain under instruction for full five years, with the option of an additional residence of three years for what is called post graduate education. They receive their preliminary training in one of the minor schools of the country, come provided with certificates of proficiency, health, and character, and are then received in the college. They have to learn Greek, Latin, English, French, German, Italian, mathematics, mental and moral philosophy, and the exact sciences. Music, vocal and instrumental, forms a large part of the program, and domestic economy is effectually taught by assigning to each of the students the several duties of managing the enormous institution.

Only a few servants are kept, and the young ladies do the rest of the work. The course of studies is a most complicated and scholarly affair, and I do not venture to deal with its details. But with all their lectures, essays, calculations, recitations, and experiments, the young ladies have to spend some of their time in the gymnasium where there are trapezes, and horizontal bars. They have boating parties of which one of them is a captain, all arrayed in long serge rowing costumes, and square university caps. The college has grounds covering more than 300 acres with a splendid lake in the middle, and gardens, woods, and shrubberies which remind one of Versailles, or some other imperial establishment. The buildings are detached, each being a palatial structure on it own basis, overlooking the grandeur of the surrounding scenery. It is entirely an undenominational institution, where every sect is equally welcomed. Divine services are regularly held, religious lectures occasionally given, and an interval of time daily set apart for private devotions in the rooms of the fair students. They are every one of them refined, elegant, lady-looking without the slightest taint of the proverbial slovenliness and awkwardness of the school girl. There are sixty-six regular teachers and professors in the College, giving instruction in every branch of learning. Of these no more than seven are male teachers, and they have charge of the minor and more insignificant parts of instruction, such as taxidermy, vocal culture, and playing upon musical instruments like the violin and violoncello. Science, mathematics, and English literature are invariably taught by ladies, almost every one of whom is unmarried. The Principal Miss Freeman is a doctor of philosophy. She is young, handsome, and most highly cultivated. I believe there are two more colleges like that of Wellesley in different parts of the United States.

Now the question comes how does all this education act towards the welfare and progressive formation of American society ? No doubt the young men are put to the necessity of acquiring at least the same standards of education as the women in sheer self-defence. But in spite of such worthy competition, I was rather surprised to learn that the most highly accomplished woman seldom falls in with the man who is likely to satisfy all her tastes. And the ordinary business man dreads to enter into the partnership of life with a woman who is esthetically his natural superior, and intellectually trained to higher knowledge. So the question of questions just now in American society is the employment of women. How are they to support themselves if they do not care to depend upon the other sex? Indian people may pooh pooh the idea of lady lawyers, and lady clergymen, lady financiers, and lady physicians. But in America all this has assumed the difficulty of an actual struggle for existence. The American people cannot, they will not retreat from the advanced position on the subject of teaching woman; the highly taught woman will not very easily choose to encumber herself with the cares and trials of domestic life. And she naturally demands every employment of life being thrown open to her. It is a curious fact that in New England and New York, the surplus of women above men is alarmingly large. And in the Western States there is scarcely one woman to six men. The result of it is that in some

States the exuberance of the luxuries and so-called refinements of life creates a morbid craving for wealth. And in other States men are so rude, manners are so harsh, revolvers and bowie knives so frightfully prevalent, that the condition of society has reverted to primitive barbarism. American households are not inferior to English households in affection and comfort, but there is an increasing number of men and women who dread household life. In some parts of the country, I am told, the horror of having too many children has produced forms of vice unmentionable in their atrocity and unnaturalness, while the extravagant habits of fine dressing and fine living are a permanent source of temptation to a great many. One is startled to see the extent to which female education has been carried in America. There are dozens of women who speak foreign languages, hold medical diplomas, write short-hand reports, edit newspapers, take photographs, and are withal as good houswives, refined, amiable, and friendly as if they had spent their whole life to learn how to make others happy. But these are individual instances. Education has not made the American woman as happy as she ought to be. And after all you can not but feel that the question of woman's elevation has not been solved in America. Some thing more than mere education needs to solve it. Nay education itself has to be tempered and educated by other influences. A great, profound, national, natural faith only can impart those influences, America needs more spiritual life. Women need more of the divine in them. May they receive that.

AMERICAN NEWSPAPERS.

It is said that a popular preacher in America was once declaiming on the furtile subject of Perdition. The horrors described fell flat upon the audience, prospect of fire and brimstone had no effect upon the hard-hearted hearers, but when the preceptor came to say that in hell no newspaper was ever allowed to be read, the congregation became deeply agitated, and the sermon was a complete success. Even in some of the prisons when victuals are reduced, exercise cut short, and various other punishments ordered, the convict is not robbed of his newspaper. Newspaper reading is simply the disease of the American. There is neither city, nor town, nor village without its newspaper. The district of New York alone publishes more dailies than England, Scotland, and Ireland put together. In all Great Britain, it is estimated there are sixty dailies, whereas in New York there are over seventy. Newspaper exchanges are despatched free by the Post Office. The newspaper is vended on the road, in the street-car, in the omnibus, in the railway train, at the church door, nay everywhere you may happen to be. The offices and printing establishments of the journals are of the finest buildings in New York. The outlay of money, some of them make, is fabulous, the enterprise is seemingly most fool-hardy. The editors hold the telegraph lines often in their hands. One of the papers is soon going to lay a private cable across the Atlantic for its own behoof. The telegraph from Europe to America be it said, outstrips the sun by about five hours, and if a newspaper has a cable of its own, it will always anticipate the occurrence of events. That is to say if an assassination, or earthquake happens in England, the *New York Herald* will publish the intelligence about four hours and half before the time the assassination really takes place. That *Herald* is a wonderful concern. It has, I believe, the circulation of half a million copies a day. It has earned lasting renown by sending Mr. Stanley to Africa to seek out Livingstone, and now Stanley has become a second Livingstone. When the Prince of Wales was in America, and went to visit the Niagra, the *Herald's* correspondent found it difficult to control the telegraphic wires, every correspondent trying to secure precedence of news. "What is to be done," asked the *Herald's* correspondent to the proprietor, "to keep the wires in our hands?" The latter immediately replied, "Telegraph the Book of Genesis." This was done, but the Prince was late, and did not arrive when it closed. "And now?" asked the correspondent. The proprietor instantly replied "The Book of Revelation." And before that telegram closed the Prince came. The strategem cost the *Herald* 700 dollars, but it beat the other newspapers out of the field. The daily newspapers are published in exceedingly small types, and contain immense quantities of information. The reporters and their staff are a race of merciless harriers and ferrets. No place and no personality is sacred to them. They dog the steps of every human being, prowl in every locality, haunt every house, pry into every secret, know and report every thing. They have attacked me at railway stations, besieged me amidst midnight stillness, collared me at the end of tiresome addresses, and buttonholed me at dinner parties. It you refuse them right information, they publish wrong information, but they must publish something. And hence the voluminous newspapers are not uniformly readable.

One great defect of American journalism is the dreadful personality habitually indulged in. There is no language too gross or violent to be used. A journal in Kentucky charged the *New York Herald's* reporter with stealing its despatches. The *Herald* replied by saying that its assailant was "an impudent one-horse Kentucky concern, conducted by a walking whisky-bottle."

The *Louisville Journal* says "the editor of the *Eastern Argus* is melancholy in his reflections on the close of the year, and says he will soon be lying in his grave. Methought he would have stopped lying when he got there. But the ruling passion is no doubt strong in death." Most people in America have heard of General Butler. He successfully led the army of the North in the Anti-Slavery War winning great renown. He was the last Governor of the State of Massachusetts. Hear how a newspaper speaks of him:—"We behold here the hideous front of hell's blackest ship, Apollyon's twin brother, the Grand High Priest of Pandemonium, the unclean, perjured, false-hearted product of Massachusetts civilization ; the meanest thief, the dirtiest knave God ever gave birth to ; total depravity personified ; that baggy-faced child of perdition Beast Butler !" Language such as this cannot promote peace and good will on earth. Hence in America editors have to fight both with the pen and the pistol. One or two have been killed. And some journalistic concerns, it is said, keep two editors on their staff, a writing editor, and a fighting editor. When the literary hero has wounded the susceptibilities of some muscular victim who comes to demand satisfaction, he is handed over to the fighting hero. And when Greek meets Greek then comes the tug of war. My friend Mr. Macrae describes a strange journalistic encounter. An Arkansas editor had enraged the roughs by a severe article on the gambling houses. Next morning when the editor was clipping copy he heard heavy steps on the wooden stairs outside, and was startled by the appearance of a big ruffian at the door, carrying a bludgeon in his hand.

"Air you the editor o' this noozpaper?" said the man.

"Do you wish to see him?" said the editor.

"I wish to see him," said the man.

"He is engaged, sir; but if you take a seat I shall tell him that you are here."

He gave the man a chair, and darted from the room to make his escape into the street. He had only got to the foot of the stairs when he encountered another ruffian just arriving, armed with a heavy cowhide.

"Whar's the editor of this here paper?" cried Ruffian Number Two, barring the way.

"You'll find him sitting in his room up there," said the editor, pointing towards the place where he had left Ruffian Number One. "But you had better not distrub him; he looks dangerous."

"I'll take that out of him mighty quick," said the man with an oath, and passed up. The editor had scarcely got into the street when he heard a terrific uproar in his sanctum, where each ruffian, taking the other for the obnoxious scribe, had begun a furious assault.

Another story is told of a Mississippi editor, who wrote a stinging article against a man who was canvassing for a public office. Next forenoon the enraged candidate appeared in the editor's room bringing with him in one hand a heavy stick, and in the other the obnoxious article which he had clipped from the paper. After a volley of oaths by way of introduction, the intruder sternly demanded of the trembling editor one of two things—either to eat his article, or take a sound thrashing. It was a painful dilemma ; but the editor chose to eat the article, and had actually swallow the piece of printed paper to save his skin.

EMERSON.

One of my first acts after arriving in America was to inquire about Emerson's home and surroundings. He lived in a picturesque little village known as Concord, not far from Boston. This Concord has a remarkable history because during the present century it has been the home of some of the greatest American minds famous in literature, philosphy, and social reform. It is the genuine Arcadia of New England, wooded, secluded, leafy, quiet, with the shadow of leisure and prosperity resting on its simple ivy-mantled home steads. It is said to have been purchased from the Indians in 1657, and soon became a great military centre. It was here that the first battles were fought between the English and Americans, and the bugle-notes of liberty were sounded for the nation. Concord is the home of that transcendental philosophy of which Emerson was the high priest.

Concord was the nursery of that fond worship of nature which gave Emerson his deepest inspiration, and found in the weird genius of Thorough a strange protest against the artificial money-loving instincts of the typical Yankee. The poetry, the literature, the heroism, the originality, and the character of America have come in a large measure from Concord. And in that village of Concord Emerson lived, laboured, and died.

I was invited by Mrs. Emerson to her house on Sunday the 2nd. September. I entered with reverent steps into the little gate on the shady roadside, the gate which, they say, is never shut. I walked over the broad marble flags to the low wide doorstep. On one side of the house is a thick mass of pines, casting their deep gloom over the study windows where Emerson wrote and contemplated. On the other side are tall stately chesnuts leading to the farm house in the rear. The whole house, which like American houses in general, is made of wood, has a most simple, unadorned, primitive aspect, giving also the idea of neatness, peace, and refinement. The library is a large square room on the first floor, with plain wooden shelves fixed in the walls containing books, not at all distinguished by their ornamental binding. Nor are the books too many, they cannot be more than a thousand volumes at the utmost, carefully chosen, and most helpful to the owner. Amongst them there are a good many translations from Persian and Sanskrit books. Emerson was notoriously fond of these Eastern treatises, specially the poetry of Hafez, and the teachings of the Bhagavat Gita. Every one knows the poem he composed in the spirit of the latter book:—

>They reckon ill who leave me out,
>When me they fly I am the wings;
>I am the doubter and the doubt,
>And I the hymn the Brahmin sings!
>The strong gods pine for my abode,
>And pine in vain the sacred seven,
>But thou meek lover of the good
>Find me and turn the back to heaven.

In the middle of the library is a large table made of mahogany, covered with papers, books and articles of literary use. The blotting pad is there, the pens recline peacefully on their rest, and a warm ornamental foot-stool of fox-skin peeps from below the cushioned seat. Every object is arranged as the sweet philosopher left it when he entered into his long repose. His widow and his unmarried daughter, with superstitious love, keep everything in its place, as if they expect his return any moment. It is awful and pathetic. Mrs. Emerson is apparently over sixty, thin, refined-looking, somewhat hard of hearing. She is a very orthodox Unitarian, different in views from her late illustrious husband. But she has a large sympathetic heart, and keeps up the celebrated hospitality of Emerson. Pilgrims from all lands and nations have been entertained in that house. The best and greatest geniuses of America there found a daily welcome.

Emerson never liked to be photographed. He never cared to waste his time to sit for a likeness of any kind. His friends say that none of the photographs extant do him any justice. The best likeness however is preserved in a marble bust to be found in Mr. Emerson's house. Those calm sunlit features always showed the profound calmness that reigned in his heart. They say he had a wonderful force, sweetness, wisdom and peace on his face. It was one of those faces on which the spirit was orbed, and lighted in all its fullness. His ardent disciples told me how Emerson used to wander alone in sunshine and starlight. He roved in unfrequented paths, and sometimes stood in the midst of his walks. He never chose to speak of himself as "I," and when it was necessary, alluded to himself he said "this person." He formed first impressions about men and things and never departed from them afterwards, but his first impressions were always correct. He loved life, and all the good and blessed things of this world. He had a singular appreciation of every form of human goodness, and the humblest and simplest often found in his house a home. He was never known to fret or fidget over any thing, and had a singularly undisturbed life. In 1873 Emerson's home was burnt down, while he was travelling in Europe. His loving and grateful fellow-townsmen subscribed among themselves to rebuild the house. And when Emerson returned, he not only found the home re-erected and refurnished, but whole Concord turned out at the railway station to welcome him back. Boys, girls, and the common people followed his carriage singing "Home Sweet Home," and saw him enter his home in joy and triumph. Emerson invited the whole village at a fete a few days after, and mutual felicitations amply repaid for the temporary misfortune.

I wound up my pilgrimage to Emerson's village by ascending the hill on the top of which he lies buried. This is the Cemetery known as the Sleepy Hollow. All the best and wisest of Concord lie buried on the hillsides. Emerson's friends, colleagues, literary acaqaintances sleep far and near around him. The trees are very tall and shady, and interweave their branches. The inscriptions are quaint, some of them exceedingly touching, several families lie in groups railed and planted round. But Emerson's grave has neither stone nor tablet over it. It is a simple mound of earth on which there is not a vestige to show whose holy remains lie beneath. Why do they not set up some memorial, however simple?

As I stood there sad and reverent, methought as if the angel stood there again, asking "Whom seek ye? He is not here. He is risen." Yet I knelt down beside the lowly mound, I kissed the cold earth where his clay moulders into dust, I broke a spray from the overhanging maple and gently laid upon the grave, I prayed that his spirit might descend upon me and my people, so that we too might behold the spirit in all things. The sweet American singer says :—

> But not beneath a graven stone,
> To plead for tears with alien eyes,
> A slender mound of earth alone
> Shall say that here a hero lies
> In peace beneath the peaceful skies.
> And gray old trees of hugest limb
> Shall wheel their circling shadows round.
> To make the scorching sunlight dim
> That drinks the greenness from the ground
> And drop their dead leaves on his mound.
> At last the rootlets of the trees,

Shall find the prison where he lies;
And bear the buried dust they seize.
In leaves and blossoms to the skies.
So may the soul that warmed it rise !

PRESIDENT ARTHUR.

I had an introduction from a prominent United States Senator to the President. I therefore ascended the marble steps of White House one fine afternoon after I had walked and driven a good deal in the picturesque metropolis of Washington. To my surprise I found a great many people had come on the same errand, and had been shown to a large waiting room where they talked, smoked, and made frequent use of the many spitoons. After a while we were ushered into the reception chamber. President Arthur stood at one end, and there were seats of all kinds placed around. The visitors walked up to him without any order or presentation, each one at the quickest opportunity, and by the shortest way. Those who were not obtrusive had to remain behind. I was seated not far from the spot where the audience was taking place, and in spite of myself, a good deal of conversation drifted away into my hearing. An aggrieved sanitarian had the President by the buttonhole, persuading him to assent to some measure of municipal reform. President Arthur tried repeatedly to shake off the eloquent reformer, but the latter as often got round, and tackled him with long complaints. At last the hard-pressed autocrat exclaimed "Now Doctor, I have heard you say that for the fourth time. Do but shorten your story." The doctor at last retreated, and another visitor approached. The absence of formality, I might even say of dignity, was startling to me after my experience of red-tapism in the Old World. Men, great-coated up to their noses, and rough-shod, and hob-nailed, came forward with their muddy boots, and extending their palms growled out "How d'e do Presden?" And the great man had to courtesy, and be affable to all. President Arthur is a tall, well-made man, past fifty, with florid complexion, scattered beard, and full fleshy face. The cares of office do not seem to have told much upon him, and he looks neither like an anchorite, nor a philosopher consuming the midnight oil. But he is perfectly goodnatured, businesslike, prosperous, patient, with a large stock of common sense at his disposal.

The President of the United States is more of of a political institution, than a personal dignitary. Men have a patriotic respect for the abstract principle of his existence; for his concrete individuality they have a tolerent familiarity which at any moment threatens to give way before a loud self-assertive equality. No President can get installed into the republican throne without a merciless ordeal of public criticism, often attended with scathing, vile, vulgar abuse. All this has a wonderful efficacy in curing him of all unnecessary airs and egotism. Amidst the levelling, undiscriminating, democracy of America, it requires extraordinary vitality of character for a man to overtop his fellows. Lincoln, Grant, and Garfield had that, the present incumbent has fairly got through his responsibilities. They say he has made a fine President, and belied the prognostications of all croakers. By the bye I might just mention I went to see the spot at the railway station where President Garfield was assassinated. A marble cross marks the point where the good man fell. I made a mental contrast with the dreary spot at Dublin Common where I stood three months before. The railway depôt at Washington was crowded to excess. Heedless feet were shuffling about the sacred spot where the faithful functionary was struck down by the traitor's hand. The environment was strangely unsuited to the act of guilt. It is a place of public resort, not of private crime. The memory of the crime is wiped out by the pressure of eager worldiness, it is strange how the dead are elbowed out by the rush of the living. Only a few months ago, spending a week at Belfast, I proceeded to Dublin. I wanted to make a pilgrimage to the spot where the two martyrs to duty Lord Cavendish and Mr. Burke, fell by the hands of the assassins. But repairing to Dublin Cathedral, I came to look at a large and fine painted window. The inscription ran thus :—" To the glory of God and in memory of Richard, the sixth Earl of

Mayo, Governor General and Viceroy of India, assassinated in the Andamans while in the discharge of duty, February 8th, 1872." I mused on this brief memorial, and all the associations of the dreadful event came back to my mind with a strange freshness. But the solemnity of the cathedral window faded before the sublimity of the bare ground on which only last year the faithful servants of Government lay bleeding and dead. Phœnix Park is an extensive place, but the spot on which the murders were committed is within hailing distance of the Viceregal residence. They fell on two sides of the narrow road in the midst of the grass. The grass has been rubbed away from the spot, and they have inscribed two wide crosses on the uncovered clay, one on each side of the pathway. The untidy Irish boys and girls were lying on the grass, and chattering to show us over the place; the costermongers were selling fruits; the women were clamouring for presents. The scene around was unfit for the dreadful memories. Strange is the mutation of human fortune, and strange the resemblance between human crimes, and human sorrows!

MRS. STOWE.

There is a singular quietness about Mrs. Harriet Beecher Stowe. One could never imagine from her personal presence that there was anything unusual in her character, or intelligence. The modesty which characterizes Mrs. Stowe is the distinctive trait of most men and women of genius I have seen in the Western world. They are observant, recipient, susceptible, more ready to take than make impressions. They unbend only before intimate friends, and are careful not to be drawn out. Mrs. Stowe had been to me a semi-mythological heroine, surrounded with a halo of romance derived perhaps from Uncle Tom's Cabin. I was therefore greatly surprised and pleased to hear that the celebrated authoress came to hear me at the Congregational Church in Hartford, which is a very interesting town in the State of Connecticut. After the service I was kindly invited to go to her house, and I responded to the request with ardor. Her home is in a retired suburb of Hartford with plenty of ground and trees about it. Mrs. Stowe is not tall, she is middle-sized, with a somewhat thin, keen-featured face in which the expressions of great serenity and benevolence enter, and cast a radiance of sweetness. She seldom laughs, she smiles, one can even scarcely say she smiles, she simply brightens all over with an inner light when she is pleased. She is at times completely absorbed in her own thoughts, remaining perfectly silent while others speak, and then she suddenly enlivens the conversation with a brilliant remark. Her interest in India is intense. She imagines however that the Hindus are somewhat like the Dacotas and Cherookees, savage, heathenish, and illiterate. And when I told her how the young men of India at one time read and wept over Uncle Tom's Cabin, she asked me whether they read it in English. Mrs. Stowe is now getting aged, and the masses of well curled hair that fell about her head, were more white than black. Professor Stowe was there with a great head of snowy hair, good humoured and jovial, but he is very deaf and infirm. Mrs. Stowe seems greatly struck by the progress of the people of India, but she does not seem to have very accurate notions of our manners and ideas.

HENRY WARD BEECHER

Is the brother of Mrs. Stowe. In the world of American theology Beecher's name is held most eminent. It deserves to be. He is a wonderful speaker and an original man. He is odd, indefatigable, magnetic, marvellously popular, and eccentric. Twice every Sunday he addresses an audience of about 2,000 people. He is seventy five years old, but never wears spectacles in day or night, and his teeth are perfect. His hair like that of Hamlet's father, is sable-silvered, but his complexion is florid, and his whole appearance like that of a man not indifferent to creature comforts. He is heard in every part of the great building where he holds his services. He never writes, but preaches his sermons extempore from notes. Nowhere outside India have I heard such prayers as Mr. Beecher offered. His style of preaching is rather sensational, but very effective.

Here are some specimens of his sayings:—
"Some people puzzle themselves about the origin

of evil. These people begin at the wrong end. What would you think of a man who, if he saw a pig in his garden, should begin to discuss the question how that pig could have got in, when the pig is busy all the time rooting up his potatoes? No; the first thing is to drive the pig out. Let us drive sin from our hearts, and from the world. Let this be our business here. We shall have a whole eternity afterwards to ascertain how it first got in." Referring to those who are great in profession, but very small in Christian activity he said, "Some men pray cream and live skimmed milk."

Again speaking of some mammon worshippers who make a profession of religion, he said "They are not satisfied with a competence, they must have it five stories high. And then they want religion as a sort of lightning-rod to their houses, to ward off the bolts of divine wrath."

Upbraiding his people on one occasion for the meanness of their contributions for the poor, he said, "There are hundreds of men here who ought to be ashamed ever to give anything but gold, or at least a dollar-bill, and they *are* ashamed to do it. Don't they, when the plate approaches, and they have put their fingers in their pockets and selected *a quarter*, use admirable tact in conveying it to the plate, so that no one shall see what they give? Pious souls! they don't let their left hand know what their right doeth. If they have two bills, one good, one bad, they will generally give the bad one to the Lord."

MY WORK IN GREAT BRITAIN.

Continuous travels for two months have given me some insight into the religious condition of this great people, and their relations to the universal cause of theism. I am thankful to acknowledge that everywhere I have met with enthusiastic and uniform cordiality. Any sympathy shown to me I claim as sympathy shown to the blessed church whereof I am a preacher. Nor has any one any cause to do me service, but to do service to the eternal principles which I spare no pains to lay before men and women. Our cause has suffered little through its enemies who have been active. Renewed confidence has been awakened in the hearts of men and women. Clouds of misrepresentation have been removed. The children of God have rejoiced to receive our message, feeling that a great light has begun to dawn upon the world. They perceive the approach and advent of the Spirit Comforter in their souls with exceeding gladness. In that gladness of trust and hope is my reward. And the fruit that my work bears will feed my own soul as reassured grace and divine strength. The Lord has been marvellously bountiful to me. I only groan in spirit at my absence and separation from friends.

The first place of any note which I visited was Oxford. In all England and Scotland there is not a prettier locality than this ancient seat of learning and religion. The omnipresent blackness of British smoke has omitted its attack on Oxford. There the cathedral spires, feudal towers, and classical pinnacles pierce into the virgin sky in all their primitive **whiteness** and airy elegance. There the most massive mighty trees arch over the roadways in lofty groves, or canopy the wide promenades in philosophical solitude. Nameless scholars lie in their lowly graves under the pavement of the gloomy cloisters alongside the college halls. The dingy cross points out where the martyrs were burnt by the bloody Bishop. And the well-worn steps of the Bodelian show what millions of pilgrims have trodden those mysterious vaults of treasured wisdom, antique art, and literary relics of all kinds. But I found my chief delight in knowing the men. Oxford at different times has formed the main artery of religious agitation. And at the present moment Oxford is the centre of intense theistic thought. The Vice Chancellor of the University, Professor Jowett, by whose kind invitation I was enabled to visit Oxford, has long been the champion of liberal thought, and Max Muller, our old well-tried friend, is ceaseless in his endeavours to bring together the East and West through the widening mediums of language, philosophy, and science of religion. Oxford men have within recent years constituted themselves into the school of theology known as the Broad Church, in whose hands in very great measure lies the religious future of England. Unfortunately in the theological organization of the West there is very little of the profound philosophy of the Divine nature except as interpreted through early Christianity. But early Christianity has little hold on Christendom. So between the absolute worship of the Son as Almighty and Infinite, and a blank utter nescience or agnosticism, there is almost no ground left for the simple rational trust in the One True God. The importance of the personality of Christ, therefore, is held with a fervid passionate tenacity by eminent Broad Church theologians. It seems to them to be the only shelter from the hungry sea of infidelity surging all around. Christ to many is the one source from which they can derive any definite certain knowledge of God. All other sources are sealed. But the merciless criticism of the age has not spared the scanty materials out of which the faith of Christendom has woven the life of the Messiah. Hence even the comfort of looking up to that life with unwavering trust is withdrawn from great numbers. And hence you will often hear some great theologian pointing out to you the path of practical usefulness as the only means of silencing the unrest and obstinate questionings of nature! Amidst all these dreary lucubrations one might expect the Unitarians to advance the affirmative standard of simple religion. Alas, they are sadly disunited amongst themselves. The organization of that small community is fast decaying, and between the fatal claims of individualism on the one hand, and the desperate attemps at uniformity on the other, there is neither repose, nor progress, nor promise for the future. My ardent good wishes and loving concern go with the Unitarians. May the spirit of God help them in their endeavours, and forward their cause. But it seems as if a rupture amongst them is inevitable. The Baptists, Congregationalists, and Independents manifest considerable life and earnestness. Some of their advanced sections present hopeful features. I have now and then received invitations to preach from Congregational ministers. Such conflicts and fragmentary activity seem to indicate that a great religious leader is the necessity of England. For a time Dean Stanley promised to be such a leader. But he is gone now, and there is no one to take his place. The purposes of Providence must in the due course of time meet with fulfilment. The hour must produce its man. The country seems to be ripe for the advent of the New Dispensation. God must raise the workers, because every denomination is more or less pervaded by ideas of the New Dispensation. In my preachings hitherto I have tried clearly to distinguish between the essential ideas and conventional expressions of the Future Religion. Rites, disciplines, orders of devotion, forms of church government must differ in different lands, communities, and nations. The harmony of essential principles is for all. I cannot but feel that up to this time I have half-uttered these great principles. The more they are uttered the more they are perceived. The more clearly they are perceived, the greater the craving to establish them unmistakably. The universal wants of the age, the universal tendencies of mankind, the growing conceptions of God, spirituality, and immortality in every religion, point to a universal system of faith. Nations will embody it according to their history, traditions, tastes. Speaking of the blessed nature of God, our relations to Him, of the facts of holiness, spirituality, future life, salvation, I have had abundant testimony of the incontestable certainty of our faith. Yet I must say the reception has been different in different parts of this kingdom. In the north of England the people are very much more enthusiastic, more susceptible, and less open to misrepresentation. You have heard of our great meetings in London and Birmingham. But there were similar meetings at Stockton, Newcastle, Manchester, accounts of which I hope have from time to time reached you. Our position in these parts of the country is as supreme as ever. Many have been the inquiries as to whether the leader is coming over again.

There is very much more to do, which he alone can do as it ought to be done.* But your humble servant feels sufficiently honored for what he has been able to accomplish. Only I wish to do more, immensely more.

In point of enthusiasm and religious fervor Scotland is far superior to England. It is orthodox, but we should like it all the more for that. There I had ministers of the straitest sects flocking to hear me, and speaking from the platform in admiration of the principles of the Brahmo Samaj. In the pretty, woody, mountainous country of Fyfe I had the pleasure of meeting with the Rev. Mr. Fyfe of the Free Church, who conferred on me his hospitality, and talked over Calcutta affairs with interest. The services at Dundee were greatly helpful to our cause. Scotland is still almost an untried field for the propagation of our religion. Very warm are the invitations I have received of going there again. The heartiness

---

* This was written in August 1883. Since then what changes have taken place in the Brahmo Samaj! Our leader and minister can no longer visit the lands that thirsted for his presence.

cordiality and sympathy of my friend, Mr. David Macrae, the Persbyterian minister, I cannot forget. But I am disinclined to mention individual names when every one has been so uniformly kind to me. On the 8th July, I crossed over to Ireland from Glasgow, and landed at Belfast. Now though Ireland is strongly Roman Catholic, Belfast is essentially Protestant.

These northern Irishmen have frequent riots, the Orangemen holding one side, and " the Papists," as they are called, holding the other. The bitterness of mutual enmity between those two classes cannot be sufficiently characterized. In Belfast, therefore, I had no difficulty in making headway. The Nationalist party here expected me to make an unsparing onslaught on the English Government. When, however, they found me giving expression to the most loyal and peaceful sentiments, setting my face most strongly against violent agitation of every kind, they were surprised, and not a few of them disappointed. But they gave me a respectful hearing, and received my mission with the warm sympathy I have everywhere found.

My chief work in England was amongst the congregations whom I addressed on Sundays and weekdays. In London alone I spoke nineteen times on subjects immediately and remotely bearing on the Brahmo Somaj, and its present situation. I willingly avoided controversies, and mainly dealt with the essential matters of the New Dispensation. But I also often entered into explanations on points which had given rise to misconceptions. On May 16th at Canon Street Hotel there was a numerous meeting of Unitarian delegates from every part of the country. In speaking of the outlook in the Brahmo Somaj I emphatically pointed out the significance of the recent developments as the necessary and natural growth of the popular side of Theism. The Oriental and Western aspects of Religion were contrasted; and it was claimed that the East had the pre-eminent right of fashioning religion according to its needs and antecedents. The freedom of spiritual instincts and national developments was demanded from a people who always upheld free speech, free conscience, and free thought. These claims met with a response which was recorded in the newspapers of the time. I made the real statement of the New Dispensation principles in London on May 27th at Hamstead before a very influential congregation in the Church of Dr. Thomas Sadler. Dr. W. B. Carpenter, Professor Drummond, and some other eminent people were present. This meeting opened me the passage to numerous other engagements. On the 1st of June the important meeting at the Memorial Hall Farringdon Street was held. The ministers of the principal denominations in the metropolis attended, and Sir Richard Temple kindly consented to take the chair. Eminent laymen, and experienced Anglo Indian gentlemen took part. It was my object at this meeting to trace the progressive series of developments in the Brahmo Somaj, and to prove that the simple monotheism of the movement was preserved in integrity amidst a many-sided growth I did not single out the misrepresentations which have been made, and I did not emphasize any particular line of thought. I presented the whole organization as it now is, and threw upon every part of it the primitive and eternal light of Theism. My critics say I dealt with the old Brahmo Samaj, and did not go into the tenets of the New Dispensation. To me the New Dispensation is the spirit, the Brahmo Samaj is the form, and it has never been, and never shall be my endeavour to separate the two. The Brahmo Somaj without the New Dispensation is mere form, name, echo, nothing. The New Dispensation is the religion, it is the light, life, glory, everything. It is for those who are against me to prove that there can be any Brahmo Somaj without the Dispensation of God. As for myself my whole mind and being are absorbed when I contemplate or descant on the dealings of God with modern India. I often forget names, persons, forms, non-essentials, cliques when I view the depths of the marvels of Providence. And throughout my operations in London and elsewhere, my humble but steadfast attempt was to illustrate as freely as I could that the good Father, the Infinite God, was unfolding a wondrous chapter of His eternal purpose in the land of the Aryans. And we in the dearth of language call that the Brahmo Samaj, or the Revelation of the New Dispensation. One great statement on the philosophy and advent of the New Faith I presented in every town I visited, so far as I now remember. It was published in Scotland, and more than a thousand copies distributed all over Great Britain. I found a most prosperous field of work in Birmingham, more so perhaps than in any other English town. More than one soul in that great town have been permeated with the spirit and life of the Divine Gospel. In Scotland I found the warmest response among a section of the Presbyterians. The congregation of the late Mr. Gilfillan, now under the Rev. David. Mecrae, a most influential and enormous body, gave me the most enthusiastic greeting. A great many ministers both of the Establishment and outside, were present, some of them on my platform. My utterances on the Dispensation of the Spirit were reproduced in the daily papers. Altogether in and about Dundee the principles of the Brahmo Samaj made true and lasting impression. My only regret is I could not stay longer to work upon this impression for abiding purposes.

A TRIP TO GERMANY.*

The Rhine.—The limits of my sketch compel me to be brief, or I would gladly describe the wonderful sceneries and objects, which ceaselessly attracted my notice during the short time I was in Germany. The Rhine, that glorious, beautiful, and romantic stream, from which the green galleried vines suck their rich life, and luxuriance,—the Rhine, over which the German soldier sang his war song as he marched to death or victory,—the castled rocks, and sunny islets of the Rhine, so full of history, and tradition, and beautiful legend, in which fact and poetry dissolve into each other in feudal and mediæval grandeur,—the Rhine itself might be the worthy theme of a writer's labour. But I must write about other things than the noble Rhine, and the great embattled cities on its banks that I have visited. Frankfort, Mayence, Coblence, and Cologne are places where the traveller may feast his eyes for months together, and there are many other cities

---

* This and the following sketches about distinguished Englishmen were written in 1874. I have revised certain passages and made additions here and there.

of minor significance. My work lay however in Wiesbaden, not on the banks of the Rhine, but a short distance from it, for at Wiesbaden the delegates of the Protestanten Varien met. The Protestanten Varien is composed of liberal thinkers from a great many religious denominations in Germany, all of whom are supported by the State. The exclusiveness and injustice of subsidizing only one section of a vast Christian community does not belong to Holland, or to Germany. Men may differ as much as they like in their religious views, and strongly avow that difference, and still continue to receive the aid of public money. To organize these various and isolated instances of independent thought into active sympathy and mutual helpfulness, the Protestanten Varien has been formed. In it there are men exactly of our own views, as well as men strictly believing in the Christian Trinity. This organization has been exsisting for the last eight years, and is certainly a great help to isolated young men who, by the boldness of their speculations, and the freedom of their faith, may be subjected to popular disfavour, and seek the communion of kindred spirits to help them onward. But no positive work is done on any recognized or common ground of union. All the work done is the annual conference at which I was present. In it there are papers read, discussions held, speeches and sermons delivered at different towns in Germany in different years. The festival lasts two days, and the eating and entertainments, all on a very grand scale, form as great an item in the proceedings, as the orations and controversies above alluded to.

Wiesbaden.—Wiesbaden is a nice little town, where invalids and fashionable visitors from all parts of Europe resort for the benefit of the mineral waters found in abundance there. There are magnificent hotels, shady walks, large handsome streets, and baths without number. And above all there is a most beautiful structure, surrounded by grounds, gardens, lakes, fountains, all of princely grandeur. This is the Kursaal. Here not long ago there was one of those gambling establishments for which at one time Germany won an atrocious notoriety. In those brilliant velvet-covered saloons, where at present some quiet, leisurely looking people are at study over the books and magazines of the month, many a princely fortune vanished, and under the blazing light of those wonderful chandeliers, men and women without number were driven to distraction, misery, and sometimes to suicide. It was in the central hall of this superb building that they spoke enthusiastic words about India, and it was here that I was invited to deliver my address on the Brahmo Somaj. The proceedings have been already published, and I need not repeat them. The festival commenced on the 28th September 1874, under the presidency of Professor Blunchley, a man of very great eminence. Though present at both the sittings of the select comittee I understood nothing, as all the speeches were in German, and the business of the first day was wound up with a concert at the Kursaal where some of the finest German music was sung and played. I found no ladies singing, in fact there were very few of them present at any of the entertainments. The few that I saw were in the Church, and I found about five or six of them at a somewhat queer place. There was a social gathering in connection with the Protestant Society, and here I went. There were about a hundred and fifty people in not a very large room, and every man had a cigar in his mouth, and a long glass of wine by his side. The smoking was without intermission, and the drinking kept pace with it, both these occupations being varied by national songs vociferated by five or six powerful Teutonic lungs, lustily cheered by the whole assembly with the applausive *Hoch!* and followed by occasional addresses, some of which, I was told, were very pathetic. The smoke dizzied my head, and I could not stay to watch whether the speeches and songs grew more pathetic or powerful as the night advanced. But I was assured all ended as satisfactorily as it had begun,—the German beer being exceedingly mild, and the German smoke innocuous. I dare say this is so, for at all the religious meetings I have been, I have found people smoking, and I have heard this is not unfrequent even during Divine service. At this social meeting I found some ladies sitting, and they were not at all disconcerted like me by the vapours and the liquids flowing around them. Thus in various proceedings the festival of the Protestanten Varien terminated. The friendly treatment accorded to me was very encouraging. I could complain of nothing. My short sojourn gave me some insight into a state of society extremely different from life in England. There are a great many points in the German character which we understand and appreciate. The heartiness, natural simplicity, and a sort of square blunt cordiality they show, are much more in our way, than the artificial refinements and cold courteseys one meets with in London. If at times the former is rough and unceremonious, the latter is as often unpleasantly elaborate and unreal. The German's respect for India is vast. And though the study of Sanscrit has not made as much progress in the country as we are led to believe, surely our classics are regarded with a romantic veneration, which will some day lead to a more extensive study. The delegates of the Protestant Union, in shaking hands with me wished long life and prosperity to the Brahmo Somaj. Let us Brahmos, in return, wish long life and success to their movement, and may it in future lead to that fraternity between them and us, the first beginnings of which may be said to have taken place nearly ten years ago.

DEAN STANLEY.*

Among those who are still in the Established Church, but whose advanced views and broad sympathies make the Brahmo Somaj a subject of deep and devout interest to them, I had the pleasure of meeting two men, Dean Stanley and Bishop Colenso. I need say very little to prove that Dean Stanley is not only a representative man in English society, but that his character and influence are sowly working a momentous change in the gigantic church organization to which he belongs. His great learning, the deep and refined piety of his beautiful utterances, his noble independence, and the subtle power of his charac-

---

* Some of these sketches, including that on Germany, were written in 1874 after my first visit to England.

ter, all impart to his heresy a charm which spreads it incessantly, while it disarms opposition. The "ethics of subscription" have been established quite on a different basis since the Dean of Westminster's views have been known; young men of restless disposition and suspicious ideas comtemplate "the thirtynine articles" in a new light, give a soothing draught to conscience, and altogether there seems to be more breathing room in the Church. Men of liberal principles, with the view of organizing themselves into a free fraternity, have now and then invited the Dean to come forward and join them. But he has always refused, and urged as the reason his want of faith in any new organization. Of course it is much more worthwhile to broaden and purify the existing church, together with all the great interests it involves, than to launch into a sectarian alliance, with strong elements of uncertainty, unpopularity, and disintegration in it. But nevertheless there is some truth in the metaphor of new wine and old bottles. And this is illustrated in the growing insincerity and anomaly which at the present day characterize the "broad" school of the Church of England. It is not always that men like Dean Stanley are to be found, and the position he occupies can, I fear, be as little understood as attained by most of the young men who profess to follow him. And in this light, I must say, that position, if it be not to a certain extent false, is certainly in a very great measure susceptible of abuse and evil. Dean Stanley's name is dear to every English theologian of the liberal school, and it ought to be dear to us of the Brahmo Samaj as well. His sympathy with our cause is open and declared, because historically as well philosophically it is a strong evidence of the truth of his own great principle. The true religious reformation of an ancient and highly-organized society is brought about, not by open defiance and hostile combination, but by quietly putting into work the natural elements of truth and spirituality inherent in it, animated and developed by the life, light, and liberty given to the world under the conditions and circumstances of modern culture.

PROFESSOR TYNDALL.

With Professor John Tyndall I had a most pleasant interview in the Royal Institution at Piccadilly. This was very soon after the great sensation caused by his address at Belfast. Professor Tyndall is a man whom after having once seen you always remember. Somewhat careless in his dress and outward manners, the result perhaps of ardent application and mental superiority, he is thin, thoughtful, and, one might say, almost sly in the expression of his countenance. In the preface to his celebrated lecture he confesses to a variation of "the moods and tenses" in his soul, and surely his face bears abundant testimony to that fact. The lights and shadows on it are very strong, and constantly changing. But underlying all, one may easily mark the seriousness and earnestness of a great mind. My conversation with him was of course exclusively on the subject in which I am mostly interested. He seemed positively unwilling to accept the usual religious phraseology. Even to the word God, if I rightly remember, he objected. The reason of this was that he fervently disapproved of the philosophical ideas attached to such words by popular theology, the reaction against which in his mind was extreme. How far in discarding these theological ideas he has discarded the essential truths of simple theism, it is not easy to determine. Only it seems logical, and therfore, in the case of a man like him, true, that holding the bold and most unequivocal creed of materialism, he cannot assent to the plain propositions as to Divine nature, and its relations with the universe, that to us are so sacred. But nevertheless, the moral enthusiasm of his nature is very great, and so far supplements the deficiency of what may be technically called religious culture, that in almost denying, or very dimly perceiving the reality of religion as an element of man's higher intellectual consciousness, he clings tenaciously to what he calls "the emotions," and out of them constructs a "Mystery," that pervades all things. From that mystery he emerges into a "Life," from that into a "Presence," and from the "Presence" into a

"Spirit," which, in the language of Wordsworth quoted by him, "impels thinking things, all objects of all thought, and rolls through all things." What he did not seem to like was to formulate into a fixed doctrine this "fluent life" and "spirit" of the universe. For my own part, I do not complain of any one coming to realize through life and emotion what I myself realize through mind, heart, and will alike; but I cannot accept the idea of a "fluent" God who has no part in the fixity of human convictions, and of the laws that regulate all things within and without. If by "fluent" is meant "progressive,"— that our ideas on the subject of God are ceaselessly growing with the growth of man's nature, I admit the word. But I admit it with the proviso that there is an element of fixity in it, an everlasting truth and certainty that ever developes and never declines, that would outlive the wreck of all false faith, and all false philosophy. I must take the liberty of observing here that Professor Tyndall's faith in this matter seemed anything but decisive. Even in my presence there seemed to be a continual ebb and flow of conviction in his mind.

The impression with which I left him was that his whole nature was glowing with a deep, vague, and transcendent sense of the Divine life, beauty, and love; but his intellect, self-bound, loyal, and logical to its creed, hesitated and failed to grasp or admit the import of that Life upon the origin, growth, and laws of being. It is a gross injustice to call him an atheist. "Working in the cold light of the understanding for many years," he said in effect to me as we rose to part, "we here *do* feel the want of the fire and vigour of that Life. It is all but extinct in England. In saying so, and in not accepting it at the hands of those who have it not, I have become unpopular. Let those who have the Life give it unto us. To you therefore in the East we look with real hope; life came from those regions once before, and it must come again. Take therefore my hearty sympathy and good will. And know that the sympathies of men like you are the few crumbs of comfort left to me in my unpopularity." On my mentioning that the morals and manners of most of our educated people were getting loose, he said the fault did not lie in the education but in the educators. "If

I had the training of your young men in my hands, whatever else they might become, I can assure you they should turn out with exalted ideas, and moral enthusiasm in their lives"

F. W. NEWMAN.

There is not a single Brahmo that will not desire to hear of their old friend and instructor, Professor F. W. Newman. He too has grown to be an old man, though his heart is as simple and sweet as it could have ever been. A plainer, more straightforward, more unworldly man I have seldom seen. He expresses his thoughts in a way that you can make no mistake about them, and he wants, if he can, to see into your's right through without fear or favor. A perfect master of language, it is dangerous to speak awhile with him, and far more to argue with him in words, about the significance of which you are in the least unsure. A foreigner as I was, in our very first interview, he pulled me up once or twice, and made me correct my meaning, and my accent. The enthusiasm and unflinching honesty of his character, led him to attempt reform wherever he found the existence of evil or abuse. He gave therefore a large, and perhaps disproportionate, amount of his time and energy to questions which did not leave him much leisure to pursue his career of religious reform, in connection with which he is so well known outside his own country. Latterly, however, I am glad to say, he has been preaching sermons to theistic congregations in London and elsewhere. His interest in the religious and political welfare of India is very great. He reads our books and articles, and watches our operations and principles with the sympathy of a brother who is concerned in their progress. It seems that nothing would cheer him more than the complete success of our work, and he listened to our aims and aspirations with a delighted sympathy which it is cheering to behold.*

CARDINAL NEWMAN.

I remember my interview with Dr. Newman at the Birmingham Oratory. "Look at his

---

* Prof. Newman has since joined the Unitarian body, and retired from public life.

brother and at that" I cried to myself after I left the venerable cardinal, and by the law of association contrasted him with his younger brother, our friend Francis William. The two brothers are as different, and yet as alike as they can be. In childlike simplicity, in honesty, firmness, and independence of character they are equal. But the elder brother is reserved, watchful, and melancholy. His whole being is absorbed in his vocation. To other demands than those of his faith, he seems to be utterly unmindful. With other men's views and principles, except such as affect his own, he seems not to have the least concern. The least shadow of a concession to satisfy any man, or even to gain any sympathy, he will not make. He holds his own with a firm grasp against a whole hostile world, and in the completeness of his mastery over his own position feels that he is secure. His security he seems to have the power to impart to others, and the Oratory over which he presides is a flourishing and peaceful place, where every thing is in order. In the sharp and dry wrinkles of his shrivelled ascetic face there is somewhere a depth of gentleness, and an expression of a sweetness which you realize but cannot describe. I was only a short time with him, but came away refreshed from the presence of a man whose hair has whitened over the maturity of his own faith, and who, in serving and worshipping, has found the peace and purity we all seek in our hearts. It matters not much to me that he is a Catholic; it is the reality of religious life I have sought in the world, and I can safely say that reality *is* in him. I have been told he is in the tenderest relations with his theistic brother, and that in losing what they both held in common at one time, they have not lost each other. And perhaps they both wait for a better union and a better brotherhood hereafter.

MAX MULLER.

I made an appointment to see Professor Max Muller at Oxford, and we had a whole afternoon together. He is rather under than above the middle height, with a face to which the utter absence of hair, together with a delicacy of complexion, gives a remarkable expression of youth. But Max Muller is by no means a very young man. He is well over fifty, if he is not ten years more. Great refinement of thought and manners, a wide and powerful intellect, and a shrewd common sense impart to his companionship a peculiar charm. He was just rejoicing at the completion of his labours over the translation of the *Rig Veda* when I first visited him. We walked together through the town of Oxford, visited the different colleges, the Bodelian Library, and different other classical spots, he walking so vigorously, and pouring upon me such a flood of information in his *naive* elegant style, that I could with difficulty keep pace either with the one, or with the other. He had some intention of visiting India in company with Mr. Grant Duff, but has subsequently given up the idea. He would be glad, he said, to wander in the streets of Benares for some years, and plunge deep into the sacred stream of Sanscrit learning as it is flowing in that ancient city. He spoke to me a sentence now and then in Sanscrit, but his pronunciation was so different from what I have been used to hear, that I could not very well understand him. We had a long talk about the Brahmo Somaj, and the position of the Conservative and Progressive parties in it. However much he may sympathize with us, his sympathy with the views and principles of Baboo Debender Nath Tagore is also great. He knew the *Pradhan Acharya's* father very well in Paris, and related to me some interesting incidents. Enlightened and advanced as Professor Max Muller's religious opinions are, his relation with the Brahmo Somaj is that of a scholar and critic simply, and nothing more. Nevertheless, to that relation he means to do full justice, and when we parted at the Railway Station, his last words were these, "Send me every information relating to your movement, every book, pamphlet, and paper; you'll not find me working always. But when my time comes,"—and then bending slightly and touching his hat, he said "Here I am."

MY WORK IN AMERICA.

America is a virgin soil for the propagation of the religion of the Brahmo Somaj. The reports of our progress and principles had dimly and vaguely reached the New World. They had heard the name of the founder Rajah Ram Mohun Roy, and the reputation of Keshub Chunder Sen had stood before them like a great shadow cast across the oceans and continents. His lectures had been now and then reproduced in the New York *Independent,* and the Rev. Joseph Cooke had done some service in spreading the knowledge of the Brahmo Somaj. At all events the information which had preceded me was meagre and unreliable. I must confess that when I crossed the Atlantic, it was with considerable misgiving, and little encouragement was first extended to me from any quarter. I landed at Boston without welcome or friend. The first greeting I obtained was in Concord, Ralph Waldo Emerson's famous village, where lived my beloved warm-hearted friend Dr. Alfred Putnam whose acquaintance I had made in England some months before. Emerson's household and all the local celebrities flocked to hear me in the Old Church. Mrs. Emerson gathered the village in her wide parlour to talk to me, as her husband had gathered them time and again to talk to many another pilgrim. My very first experiences were of the *veni, vedi, veci,* order. To quote from my diary dated August 31st. :—

"Well begun is half-done. God be thanked I have really commenced well. On the very first Sunday of my American sojourn I have addressed an intelligent audience. This is more than I could have expected. My mind is easy and faithful. If Providence grants me health and fervency of spirit, I will cheerfully go through my appointed work. I depend upon Him and Him alone. I am asked to attend the meetings of an influential society."

This society is the Social Science Congress of America. I was invited to be a guest of the Society at its annual meetings in Saratoga. Saratoga is a fashionable watering place in the United States, about a hundred miles from Boston. There are extensive mineral springs, and palatial hotels there. The wealth, the intellect, and the aristocracy of America gather at the Saratoga springs towards the end of summer. And to Saratoga I went in the beginning of September. During the three or four days I delayed there, I was made to work almost incessantly. The Society held three sessions daily at each of which I was obliged to speak. As soon as the regular speeches were over half a dozen men waited to besiege me with 'questions" on my way from the platform to the gate. And when fagged and overworked I reached my hotel, there the ladies waited on the piazza with graceful smiles, and asked if it would be too much for me to give them "a talk, a *mere talk* you know,' in the parlor! I often yielded to these requests. But the state of my brains and nervous system soon warned me to be careful. I saved myself by sheer running away. But though I had to work overtime, the Saratoga meetings served me with golden opportunities of introduction.

Men from every corner of America had gathered there, and I made friendships which were of incalculable importance to me afterwards. At Saratoga I did not make more than two or three *religious* speeches, one of them being on the subject of our Church. The rest were social and general statements. But a great deal of interest in India was roused, and invitations began to pour in from every town. Returning to Boston on the 7th September, the first engagement I made to preach was in a Congregational Church of the first eminence in that city. Dr. J. Duryea is a scholar, philosopher, and reformer in the congregational body, and when he invited me to speak from his pulpit, and Joseph Cooke undertook to introduce me, there was no lack of audience. All denominations gathered, and my friends the Unitarians did not at all take it amiss, but congratulated me that my first public appearance was not in their church, but in an orthodox one. Venerable, gentle Dr. W. Freeman Clarke was there, and immediately afterwards asked me to preach from his pulpit. These engagements so far satisfied public sentiment, and the leading newspapers of Boston so well reported me, that the people determined to confer upon me the honor of a public reception. In the Hotel Vendome the principal place of public resort in Boston, I witnessed an assembly of the leading men of the city, who gladly listened to my message. A little while before this meeting the Institute of Unitarian Ministers invited me to address them at Lowell, a manufacturing town not far from Boston. There the impression made by our principles was so strong, that they in a body presented me with their testimony as to the purity of my cause, and exercised their influence to secure me an extensive and influential hearing. Thus day after day progress was made in my work.

After staying awhile the sphere of my work enlarged in America. One powerful auxiliary I found was in the publication of my book the Oriental Christ. I was graciously accorded an opportunity to bring out before the public this treatise which I have been writing for more than the last two years. The Oriental Christ which was very favourably received in certain quarters excited more attention than ever to the Dispensation of the Brahmo Somaj. And as I left Boston for other towns, I found that a universal greeting awaited me everywhere. In the great city of New York where it is so difficult to find a hearing my meetings had been bespoken. And both there and at Brooklyn I spoke more generally from orthodox pulpits than from Unitarian pulpits. They willingly and liberally contributed towards my necessary expenses. And I can quote no better testimony of sympathy with my work than this. An Episcopalian congregation, that of the Rev. Heber Newton, helped to procure for me a free first class passage both by railroad and steam ship from New York to Hong Kong, a distance of over ten thousand miles through land and sea. No community and no church had any deep objection to the principles and attitude of the New Dispensation. And as to its spirit, they hailed it with acclamation. If it be the chief negative work of the Brahmo Somaj to remove sectarianism, this unsectarian greeting, this unanimous welcome given to our principles, ought to be the cause of the greatest encouragement. The transcendent truth has been established that the religion of Divine Fatherhood and human brotherhood has met with universal recognition. The results of this recognition will develop more and more fully as time passes on. My only regret is I could not make a longer stay. From Boston to San Fransisco my experiences have been the same. With Weslyans, Independents, Episcopalians, my experiences have been the same. The atmosphere of America is ripe for every influence of the New Dispensation. In our movement they behold the rise of a universal light which will gladden all mankind. I feel nervous and loth to write lest it should seem that in saying all this I am blowing my own trumpet of praise. I know my work could have been better executed, I am conscious of a hundred omissions. But it would be ingratitude on my part to conceal the feeling that my lobours have been more than amply rewarded. I feel blessed in my work. I have done my duty, I have established my cause—Glory be to God, and in His church be peace, progress, and good will.

THROUGH THE PACIFIC TO JAPAN.

Across the great Pacific, from San Francisco to Japan it is 5,200 miles. The Pacific mail steamers have two prescribed routes one for summer, traversing the north, through high winds and heavy seas, and the other for winter, traversing the south, within twenty degrees of the equator, where the winds are mild, and the waters less boisterous. Leaving California on the 22nd November, when the snow was already beginning to pile on the high lands of the Sierra Nevada, we of course took the southern route. The Pacific is a very uninteresting ocean, the only singular thing about it being that it was ever called *Pacific*. True the Atlantic gales were absent; but the wonderful atmospheric marvels of the Atlantic, the calmness, the sunshine, the haze, and the transparent sky were also absent. Where were the mysterious petrels, wheeling gulls, playful porpoises, spouting whales? Where were the specks on the horizon, crawling nearer every moment, found to be sails at last, fellow-pilgrims on the wilderness of the waters, moving with us on the face of an all-encompassing eternity? The Pacific howls and rolls, rises and hollows, threatens squalls, holds forth rains, and is full of gigantic tricks. The only interesting object one beholds is just outside the San Franciscan harbor, known as the Golden Gates, I mean the two seal rocks. Rising sharp and abrupt out of the ocean these rocks furnish shelter to hundreds of seals, or as they are called sea-calves. These animals are unwieldy, of a dubious brown which, when dry, becomes dirty white. They are heavily mostached, small-eyed, stupid to a degree, keeping up a perpetual hubbub, halfway between a bark and a bray. You see them basking, plunging, climbing, jumping, and in all conditions of rude titanic gambols. Another interesting feature of the Pacific voyage is the abolition of a day. Can you think of a week without a Tuesday? Yet it was our unpleasant duty to drop off Tuesday the 4th December from our almanac. The fact of the matter is that when we reached the 180th parallel of longitude, where the world stands geographically halved, to keep ourselves even with the rest of mankind in point of time, we had to drop a day. We were at that point now when our Tuesday would be the world's Wednesday. Nor could we say whether we were East or West on the map, we were on the central line between what men call the East and West, every thing to the East, and every thing to West. This pilgrimage round the earth, sets at their real value a great many human calculations, and we find after all we are very conventional beings. Time and space are eternal, we measure them in our small poor way. It took us full twenty days to cross the Pacific and as we stood on the deck of our fine ship the "City of Peking," on Wednesday the 12th December, we sighted the hilly coast-line of *Dai Nippon* (Great Land of the Sun) commonly called Japan. Once more to cast my weary looks on the sacred continent of Asia, was like catching a glimpse of my dear long-lost home. And as the ship drew near land, there was the feeling as if I crept near to a mother's bosom. That night about ten o' clock, we cast anchor in the beautiful harbour of Yokohama. We had to sleep on board impatiently watching for daybreak. Early in the morning the Grand Hotel steam launch, and native sampan boats, came to take us on shore. It was bitterly cold, a raw damp wind penetrated every protection, and defied every fold of clothing. Muffled, strapped, gloved, greatcoated we set out, and after half an hour's steady sail, jumped on the slippery rocky landing. The first objects that invited our attention were ruddy, sturdy, copper-coloured shortsized human beings who offered to take us, wherever we might like to go, in their ginirickshaws. You know what the ginirickshaw is. It is a giant perambulator, or miniature buggy. "It is a baby carriage on adult wheels." It holds one or two. It has a hood and shafts, and is dragged by a man instead of a pony. Sometimes you may employ two men, one before, one behind. It is the cab, the hack, the ferry, the pulman car, in fact about the only public conveyance you have in Japan. What the jhampan is on the Himalaya Hills, what the buggy is in Bombay, the tonga in Poona, the ekka in Allahabad, the gondola in Venice, the street-car in Boston, that is the giniricshaw in Japan. It must have been invented by some European or American, when nobody knows. It is cheap, expeditious, and clean. The men who draw the ginirickshaw are models of health; some of them wear their hair most elaborately curled and combed, their feet encased in padded socks sometimes soled with straw. Some of them are well clothed, others have as much clothing as the harness of the horse. They run at the rate of three miles an hour, I fully believe. Some of them speak English, all of them are polite and obliging.

Yokohama is on a hilly coast, though the sea-front is level enough. The principal residences are on a hill known as the Bluff. The population is mixed, both native and foreign, the natives being generally shopkeepers and others of the lower orders, though some of them are also clerks and officials. The roads are wide and large, and the houses though without much distinct character or style, are some of them stately and handsome. The hotels and foreign consulates have the best buildings. The Japanese government has an imposing building for their court house. So late as 1853 Yokohama was but a small fishing village, with a few hundred inhabitants. And now it is a great stately city with nearly 15,000 people, its harbour studded with the shipping of every nationality, its importance rising. The opening of Japan to the commerce and civilization of the world is the secret of the prosperity of Yokohama.

WHO ARE THE JAPANESE?

Are they a simple primitive race like the Chinese? Are they the compound of several streams of nationalities? Many well-informed men have set themselves to answer these questions. Whatever may be the details and processes by which they come to a conclusion, one thing is certain. The Japanese are not a simple race. Their language, their traditions, their religions, their customs, their personal appearance, and physical peculiarities prove that they are the result of a fusion of races. This fusion must have taken place unnumbered centuries back. But the stock from which the Japanese have mainly sprung is still existent. These are known as the *Ainos*. They are said to be the aborigines. They still abound in Northern Japan, Jeddo, and some of them are even to be seen in the neighbourhood of modern towns. They are short, thick-set, hairy men, considerably ignorant and rude, compared to the Japanese of to-day. But they are very free from the well-known Mongolian features and traits of character. Some say they originally came from India. Their personal appearance certainly favors that supposition. If these *Ainos* are the basis of Japanese nationality, the other races which mixed themselves with it were undoubtedly the Chinese, the Coreans, the Malays, and the various waifs and strays of south-eastern Asia. As a matter of fact you find in Japan two very distinctive and widely conflicting orders of features. You often notice the highly oval Mongolian face, prominent cheek-bones, delicate rose-tinted complexion, oblique eyes, long drooping eye-lashes, the well chiselled fine-cut features of the Chinese aristocracy. These traits are peculiarly noticeable among the women. And then you find the square muscular forms, the massive necks, the short thick noses and ears, the bearded hairy faces, eyes at right angles with the nasal bridge; the bull-necked or absolutely neckless men and women, whose swarthiness and coarseness of physiognomy at once prove that they are of a different origin. In all Japanese works of art—vases, dishes, toys, screens, and fans, these distinctive types of face are unmistakable. But there being absolutely no caste in Japan, these types are every day becoming more and more homogenous.

It is a disputed point whether there has been any indigenous literature in Japan. When the intercourse between that country and China first began the Japanese were very ignorant. As a matter of history we discover that the earliest composition of literary works was attempted in the Chinese character, and according to Chinese grammar and forms. Considering the distance of the two countries and the great difference of manners, local idioms and colloquial phrases soon crept in, thus giving rise to a distinct dialect which in the course of time has taken the shape of the modern Japanese language. The importation of Buhdism from China also tended in a great measure to perpetuate the importance and integrity of the Chinese classics. And even at the present day the Budhistic vocabulary of Japan forms a sort of intermediate dialect half-way between the Chinese and Japanese tongues. Another influence has strangely modified the formation of Japanese literature. The wonderful progress of Roman Catholic Christianity in Japan in the seventeenth century has given a tincture both to the written and spoken language of the people. Western missionaries, who now translate Japanese literature, are struck with pieces of Christian phraseology bodily interwoven in it, coming across such expressions as " the vale of tears," " gone to his reward," "dust and ashes," &c. Nothing determines the destiny of a language so much as religion. All human expressions, deep thoughts, obstinate beliefs, have their origin in religion. When therefore it is stated that for centuries together Buddhism and Christianity have directed the national life of Japan, one can easily think that the literature of that country will bear to each of these two religions the relation proportioned by the influence it has had to form the life and the manners of the people.

THE RELIGION OF JAPAN.

The religion of Japan now, and for a long time, has been nominally divided between Shintoism and Budhism. But practically it has been Budhism. Competent authorities who have discussed the subject refuse to recognize Shinto as a religion. It is a political creed which enjoins divine honor to the Emperor, to ancestors, and to heroes. It also enjoins many ceremonies and forms of personal purification It is composed of a vast number of small deities whom the people worship according to their needs. "In its higher forms," says Griffiths, "Shinto is simply a cultured and intellectual Atheism. In its lower forms, it is blind obedience to governmental and priestly dictates. Strike out the doctrine of the divinity of the Mikado, and almost nothing is left of modern Shinto but Chinese cosmogony, local myth, and Confucian morals." One may not agree with this estimate. No mere myth and cosmogony can hold the faith of a nation for centuries. I have seen Shinto temples. They bear the emblems of a *polished miror* and *a brush*. The one is to me an adequate representation of the spirit of Him in whom all the universe and every soul discover their true lineaments. The other is the typical embodiment of self-purification. There are touching sacraments connected with these shrines which prove that Shintoism at one time held a powerful sway over the feelings and convictions of the people. But without doubt Shintoism could not cope with Budhism in philosophical depth, or principles of personal sanctity. It is said that in the 7th century of the Christian era Budhism first found its way into Japan. The Japanese are a simple people. Debaucheries and carnal excesses never characterized them. They are a law-abiding peaceful people, though they have not shown themselves deficient in courage and heroism. They are also a subtle and intelligent race. Hence the personal purity, the moral precepts, the ecclesiastical organization, and complicate laws of the early Budhistic church found in Japan a fertile field. Whole tribes accepted the great faith. Missionaries travelled into the country from China, Corea, perhaps even from India. Many sects of Budhists were founded. Now and then there was persecution, but that only compacted the new organizations. In the course of time the powerful chiefs made it their religion. Budhism reached its culmination in Japan in the thirteenth century of the Christian era. Sects were founded about that time which still retain their power. In the popular embodiments of Budhism the purity of Sakya's doctrine has fled. It is a many-headed polytheism, male and female, allied to Shintoism, allied to Christianity, the reigning symbol over every thing being the lotus-flower. Amita Buddha sits on that flower of many petals. The flower is the emblem of the complicated laws of Sakya. It is significant of the complex priesthood also. The simple people approach the elaborately carved and lacquered altar. They make their *namaskar*, and bow their heads as we do in India. The formula they slowly utter is " *Namu Amita Buddha.*" Salutation to thee O eternal Buddha. The reformed formula of worship, as now practised, is somewhat different, it is "*Namu mio ho renge kio.*" Salutation to the salvation-bringing lotus of the book of laws. The Budhist priesthood is held in great veneration. A large number of them are most humane and holy in their lives. According to one of the sects the priest can marry, but generally they have to remain celibate. The majority of them never eat any animal food. The Japanese principally live on rice and a little fish. It is only very recently after the example of the foreigners, that they have learnt to have a liking for beef, and other kinds of European food. It is altogether false that they eat cats and dogs. Far from that, it is often a difficult thing in Japan to procure meat of any kind. During all my wanderings in Yokohama and Jeddo I did not meet with a single butcher's shop. The people live on rice, vegetables, and some fish when they can get it. They even abjure milk and butter. They are one of the most abstemious races on the face of the earth.

JAPAN MODERNISED.

Japan has come to be the Eldorado of Asia. Romantic reports of its progress and aspiration fill the atmosphere. The land of the rising sun (*Dai Nippon*) seems somehow to be the land of hope in our continent. This perhaps is on account of the prevalence of European tendencies amongst us. Politics, manners, costumes, ideas, virtues, vices are all taking a new form in the model of European civilization. Yet after all, to an impartial observer, it would not seem that Europe has penetrated more into Japan than India. Undoubtedly our people have been greatly more occidentalised. But Japan is a free country, a comparatively new country, and the Japanese people have a good deal of strong national feeling. The world at large takes more interest in a free country whose people go forward by their unforced, independent will, than in a country like India where the will of the conqueror is the law of the subject race. Hence on the whole modern Japan has more reputation for progress than modern India. Yet thirty years ago who ever spoke of Japan? There was a powerful, feudal aristocracy, stagnant, priest-ridden, exclusive, with a deadly abhorrence of all foreigners. Less than a hundred years ago Christianity was fearfully persecuted, and had all but ceased to exist. Every province was under the dictatorship of a feudal chief, or *daimio*, who was very nearly independent and defiant of the sovereign power. He had hordes of military retainers, and a following of desperadoes that were the dread of all orderly people. The *daimio* occasionally visited Jeddo the capital. Seated on horse-back, or on an exalted chair, he moved about in procession, his followers both on foot and horseback going behind him. Any one who crossed the path of the procession was attacked, oftentimes killed. In September 1862 one Mr. Richardson, with two other gentlemen and a lady, rode into the neighbourhood of the procession of the *daimio* of Satsuma. They were warned of their danger, but Richardson with the temerity of an Englishman said "he knew how to deal with such people" The party galloped into the procession. The Japanese taking this to be a deliberate insult, immediately fell upon the intruders, and without hurting the lady at all, inflicted serious wounds upon the men, of which Richardson died. In consequence of complications arising from this event a fleet of English warships attacked a Japanese port called Kagoshima, bombarded the place, fired the houses, and slaughtered thousands. The Japanese fought with obstinate valor, but could do nothing against the superior arms and tactics of the invaders. This encounter, while it shows the popular hatred of foreigners, may be taken as one of the circumstances which brought Japan under the direct operations of European influence. Though defeated the Japanese did not cease to hate, but hated all the more "the foreign barbarians" And the development of the present attitude of semi-Europeanism in Japan is therefore an interesting study.

For centuries, dating perhaps from the twelfth, there was a dual form of Government in

Japan. There was the Mikado, who was admitted on all hands, to be the legitimate ruler of the land. And there was the Tykoon, or Shogun, who was a sort of commander-in-chief to the Imperial forces, the supreme military power of the realm. In the course of time, with the degeneracy of the line of emperors, the Tykoon came to usurp more and more authority, till virtually he became not only independent, but the actual ruler of the country. The Mikado or Emperor lived in Kioto, the Tykoon in Jeddo. Both of them had separate courts and counsellors. Each provincial lord under such example also assumed local sovereignty; and Japan was torn up by a multitude of feudal factions that often came to fight in desperate enmity. But over these all there reigned the Mikado, the nominal Emperor, and the Tykoon, the military despot of the land. In the course of time there came to be formed two leading parties, one of which, in view of the usurpation and the tyranny of the Tykoon, favored the restoration of the Mikado into full power. They insisted that the Tykoon should revert to the state of a mere vassal of the State which he really was. The other party, conscious of the opportunity which such a divided rule gave to personal ambition, became the strong adherents of the Tykoon, ready to go to war for his sake. This had remained the political condition of Japan for long years, when in 1853 a fleet of American ships steamed up the Bay of Jeddo, and anchored where the modern city of Yokohama now stands. For a long time the Japanese had regarded these black ships of "the foreign barbarians" with suspicion and hatred. They felt there was danger in store for them there. And when Commodore Perry appeared with his fleet before Japan 1853, a good deal of agitation was consequently felt. The authorities directed him to go to Nagasaki, the only port then open to foreign vessels. But Perry refused. He said he had despatches, and presents for the Emperor which he wanted to deliver. To whom was he to deliver them? The Mikado was living with his court, such as he had, far away in Kioto. The Tykoon was at hand, only ten or twelve miles from the sea, holding his council, and exercising supreme authority at Yeddo. And the Tykoon took upon himself the responsibility of dealing with Commodore Perry, entered into a treaty, and then sent the papers to the Mikado for formal sanction. This greatly enraged the Japanese people, firstly because the legitimate position of the Emperor was ignored, and secondly because the hated "foreign barbarians" were admitted into the country by the Tykoon's self-seeking policy. The party in favor of the Mikado became very much strengthened by this circumstance, and the foreigners became if possible more hated than before. Then began the outrages upon individual Europeans, culminating in the Richarson affair described before, which caused the bombardment of Kagoshima in 1862. The next year 1863 another Japanese port Shimonosaki was bombarded. This time the attacking fleet consisted of English, American, French, and Dutch ships, all united to humiliate the power of Japan, and prove to her that she had no choice but to yield to the pressure of foreign demands. These two bombardments effectually impressed the Japanese of the superiority of Western power. The defeat suggested to them the necessity of learning in

Europe and America the modern art of warfare.

In the meantime the chronic conflicts between the parties at home culminated. The Mikado was favored by the foreigners. The Tykoon's influence daily waned. The Mikado was for progress, for education, for commerce, the Tykoon was for exclusivism, feudal power, and the ignorance and conservatism of ages. Young men were secretly sent to foreign countries by the Mikado's party such as England, Holland, and America to learn the sciences. The power of the feudal aristocracy was denounced, and attempts were made to curb it. At last the two parties came to an open rupture in 1868. The Tykoon's forces were signally defeated. The Mikado became the only supreme power. The Tykoon's office was abolished. The seat of the Empire was changed from Kioto to Jeddo, and the name of Jeddo was changed into Tokio.

The successful bombardment of Kagoshima and Shimonosaki led the foreign powers to demand a revision of the treaties, and one of the conditions exacted was the opening of certain ports to European commerce. Americans and all classes of traders from Europe poured into Japan, and the people saw the unquestionable advantages of such an open communication. 'All the impressibility of the Japanese character came in to foster new aspirations, and visions of future prosperity, so here was a real inducement for imitating Europeans. The revolution of 1868 which concentrated all power in the Mikado, and abolished the feudal aristocracy of the Tykonate, brought in a new race of men into power. They were young, well-educated, partiotic, and radical in their politics. My friend Mr. Arinori Mori, the Japanese minister in London, was one of them. They counselled the Mikado to establish a Council of State. The young emperor then only sixteen years old, came personally to open the Council, took his oath as ruler of the land, and promised "that a deliberative assembly should be formed ; all measures decided by public opinion ; the uncivilized customs of former times should be broken through ; and the impartiality and justice displayed in the workings of nature be adopted as basis of action; and that intellect and learning should be sought for throughout the world, in order to establish the foundations of the empire."

This declaration, somewhat highflown as it is, is the basis of the present order of things. The internal conflict completely ended in 1870. But the new machinery of Government did not work well. The damios or provincial chiefs still had some following. There was a race of wandering warriors, known as Ronins, utter desperados, idlers, wash-bucklers, who carried their lives in their hands, and girded themselves with three swords, which they used at every real or imaginary provocation. They were the inveterate haters of all "foreign barbarians." Other measures were necessary in order that the principles of the new revolution might work well. So in 1871 a number of patriotic chiefs memorialized the Emperor to the effect that they, and others like them, might make over the lands they held from the crown to the crown again, and retire into private life. According to the spirit of this memorial an edict was sent to all the feudal chiefs, and obeyed by them. Hundreds of offices were abolished. The three-sworded Ronins were deprived of their weapons, and commanded to till the ground. Schools, colleges, and universities were established. Missionaries from all countries flocked into Japan. Japanese students were sent in increasing numbers to the centres of learning in Europe and America. Books on western manners and customs were translated into the vernacular by patriotic scholars. The people read Smiles's Self Help, Mill's Essay on Liberty, and Herbert Spencer's First Principles in their own language. And as a crowning measure to all this, the celebrated Japanese Embassy was organized, and sent to all the civilized courts of the world in 1872. English and Amrican professors were invited, the youngmen began to learn mechanics, engineering, shipbuilding, and other important arts. They filled their own dockyards, manned and organized their own ships, and are now slowly replacing the fereign professors in their colleges and schools.

Such is a short history of the modernization of Japan. The process is not more than thirty years old, and the question now comes how is all this to end. That Japan has thrown herself into the comity of nations there is no doubt. But can she make or retain her position? Unfortunately up to this time Japan has neither enough of foreign civilization nor enough of sturdy nationality. And between the two principles, the nation presents painfully unsettled prospects. The national ideals differ greatly between the handful of the educated, and the great body of the people. The former are more or less radical, disposed to advocate the political fashions of America and England. According to the instincts of the people, all virtue and all religion reside in absolute obedience to the sovereign of the land. The scholars trained in foreign countries are profoundly opposed to all traditional ideas, and yearn for the day when their own agnosticism will permeate the masses. On the other hand the few offices still held by foreigners are regarded with ill-concealed jealousy by the rising generaton. One great grievance felt by the better classes is the ex-territorial clause of the foreign treaty which excludes Japanese magistrates from trying criminals belonging to other nations. Japan wants to shake off the foreigners without having sufficiently mastered the elements and principles of foreign civilization. Under these circumstances it is difficult to believe that the progress of the country will be as steady and as effectual as to make it a foremost example to Asiatic nations. The Japanese are such an industrious, happy-tempered, susceptible race, that it will always sufficiently interest the rest of the world, and especially India. But then no part of India and no part of Asia has ever been satisfied with the hollow forms of mere outward refinement. Politics, commerce, and ship-building, the manufacture of paper, silk, and lacquer may be good, but no nation could ever make a mark on the world by these. Mankind look forward to higher concerns. Religion and philosophy, great examples of character and self-sacrifice are indispensable towards the formation of a people. Of these the Japanese don't seem to feel any need yet. Their happy go-lucky ways, and the occasional approbation of the world are to them a sufficient guarantee that they are on the right track. Time alone, and deeper perhaps sadder experience shall develop greater solidity and greater dignity than one meets with in Japan just now. One thing is certain. It is of the utmost consequence that enlightend men from different countries, specially from Asiatic countries, should visit this interesting people, and impress them with principles which, both in the East and the West, have gone to build national life upon ever-lasting progress in truth, righteousness, and spirituality.

JEDDO OR TOKIO.

Yokohama is connected with the metropolis by a narrow gauge railroad. It is only one hour's journey, and all the way equally interesting. There are thick patches of pine and cedar, skirted by well-irrigated rice-fields. There are prosperous villages, with thatched and tiled residences, all surmounted by the concave arcs which distinguish the architecture of Japan and China. About six miles outside of Yokohama there is a well-built settlement, consisting apparently of many hundred houses, all in the same style, with balconies round them, story after story hung with lanterns, and kept in good order. This is the quarter to which all women of questionable reputation are driven from the town proper. The houses are owned by proprietors, and the residents, who are helpless creatures huddle in together, supervised and controlled by the authorities. The general look of the country to a Hindu, who has travelled in Europe and America, does not seem to be very outlandish. There is an oriental, familiar, homely air about it all, with the crops lying on the ground, the hay-stacks on the way side, the men, women, and children (curiously dressed) standing near the houses to catch a glimpse of the passing train. The Buddhist and Shinto temples loom in the distance, and the peasants are going about with burdens on their back. At last Jeddo is reached. The capital has changed its name since the change of Government in 1868. It is no longer Jeddo, now it is *Tokio*. Tokio is a large city of one million souls. It is extensive, and closely built. All the foreigners are obliged to live by themselves in a quarter called Tsukiji, where there are proper defences for them against any outrage from the people. Because it ought to be remembered, that so recently as fifteen years ago, the life of an Englishman or American was anything but safe in Tokio. One singular feature of the Japanese town is the absence of cattle in the streets. There are very few horses, and fewer still of bullocks. I saw some soldiers and officers riding ponies, but not a single horse. Even the ponies I was told were imported. I saw two bullocks only in two days, drawing carts. Men are so plentiful that they do everything. Another feature is the absence of head-dress among the people. It was exceedingly cold, the thermometer, I believe, at less than forty, but every man and woman went about bare-headed, except those who fancied European hats. Both sexes combed their hair most elaborately, the women constructing regular pagodas on their heads, while the men contented themselves with thickly swelling curling ram's horns. The elderly and old fashioned cut their hair into three top knots, shaving the interspaces, and tying up the masses in a triangular crown, the central knot higher than the other two.

It will be difficult to give an adequate idea of the Japanese costume. It is very involved, loose, arranged layer after layer in different dimensions, black, blue, purple, striped, ending in a pair of wooden shoes or clogs fully five inches high. The outer choga is short, with immense loose sleeves. They have a trick of coiling and sticking out their arms inside their dress, which gives you the idea that as a nation their hands are all amputated, and they carry nothing but stumps covered by those capacious sleeves. They hobble with the absurd clogs underneath their feet, and when in the paved streets, or floored railway stations a number of them walk fast, the hubbub and clatter they make render it impossible for you to hear anything else. The women are exceedingly short but really handsome. Unfortunately as soon as they marry they have to shave their eye-brows, and blacken their teeth. Their dress is very picturesque leaving a considerable part of the body below the neck open, as well as the hands up to the elbows. But a great many men have adopted the European dress. The soldiery and the police are all arrayed in ill-fitting trowsers and jackets, the caps too big for their heads. The policemen have contracted a great fancy for green spectacles. Being undersized men, with long sabres stuck in their belts, it is quite a sight to see them stalking about uncomfortably in their pork-pie hats, heavy steel scabbards, and fashionable green glasses! I never saw a tall man in Japan, I never saw a man with luxuriant beard or mostache. Amongst the better classes I never saw a stout or muscular figure. They are slight, dwarfish, and parched up about the face. But they are wonderfully good tempered. Every one is cheerful. Nay the absence of dignity is a characteristic feature of the Japanese mental constitution. I cannot say I was struck with the solidity of the nation. Yet there is no question that the Japanese are a brave people. Nay their fierceness a few years ago was proverbial. Every gentleman amongst them carried a couple of swords underneath his dress. And on the slightest provocation not only drew them, but recklessly thrust them into the offender, be he who he might. It was with difficulty that this pugnacity could be put a stop to. But now they are the most courteous and good-tempered of nations. It takes an effort to believe that underneath this exuberant politeness there lurks the fierce irritability of a proud temperament. The soldiers in appearance are very like our Gurkhas; but the policemen in long sabres and green eye-goggles seem like over-grown babies dropped down from some strange planet. The wonderful elegance of Japanese workmanship is known. They excel in porcelain work, paper work, ivory carving, and ornamental lacquer. I saw some wonderful specimens. I found whole temples, walls, and altars lacquered in gold and bronze of marvellous splendor. In cunning workmanship on paper and porcelain no European nation can excel them. In substantial art however they lack very much. They paint beautifully on fans, screens, mats, and vases, but I did not see a single real framed picture of any artistic value. The buildings too lack in finish and style. The only grand structures I saw were the temples, stone-lanterns, pagodas, and spires. But I do not know how far they are the peculiar productions of Japan. They seem to be imitations of Chinese edifices. But so far as they go, no doubt they are exceedingly fine.

The Japanese go in for a considerable amount of school education. The total number of government schools was 30,779 with 77,465 instructors in them. These schools are interspersed throughout the country, and impart instruction to something like 2,271,850 boys and young men. Besides these there are about 2,000 other schools where the prescribed course of study is departed from for local reasons. Over and above these there are what they call professional schools, where foreign languages and other subjects are taught. There are three schools for the dumb and blind where the number of admissions is continually on the increase. There is a gymnastic institution where the young are taught athletic excercises, and there are five Kindergartens for children where the most recent improvements of the system have been introduced.

The Tokio University, under the control of the Government, comprises four departments, Law, Medicine, Science and Literature. The number of students is a little over two hundred. The instructors are Japanese as well as foreigners, of whom there are fourteen just now. The course of study is at the longest for five years, and the education given is thorough and sound. The Japanese Government sends a number of its promising students to foreign countries, such as America, England, Germany and France. These men after their return fill the exalted offices under the State, and enlighten their fellow countrymen. Altogether education in Japan has a scientific and practical character. Not the least mention is made in the educational reports of any religious instruction, though morality is strongly recommended. The Minister of education in his published "directions for the teachers of elementary schools," thus begins :——

"To lead men to be virtuous is more important than to make them intelligent, and consequently teachers shall direct their special attention to moral education, and make the scholars loyal to the Imperial House, patriotic to their country, filial to their parents, reverent to their superiors, faithful to their friends, merciful to their inferiors, self-respectful, and so forth, that they may well understand the great principles of human relations. Also the teachers, standing in the position of constant examples to the scholars, shall endeavour to imbue them with moral principles, and to influence them by their own good conduct.

The object of intellectual education is to enlarge men's knowledge and to develop their mental faculties, that they may be able to discharge their proper duties, not for the vain purpose of gaining renown or seeking after the achievement of extraordinary deeds."

JAPANESE WISDOM.

The wisdom of Japan is concentrated in fine proverbs which Mr. Griffiths has translated. I quote a few below:—

Who can scatter a fog with his fan?

Even with too many boat-men, a boat cannot run uphill.

The fortune-teller cannot tell his own fortune.

He can argue till the crow's head becomes white.

A bigot looks at heaven through the needle's eye.

The wily cat is like a hermit in the market-place.

The dilatory man seeing the lion begins to whet his arrows.

Fighting sparrows fear not man.

By losing gain.

Give opportunity to genius.

To give riches to a bad man, is to give an iron club to the devil.

While the hunter looks afar for birds, they fly and escape at his feet.

The beautiful woman is unhappy.

A calamity, left alone for three years, becomes a good fortune.

Birds flock on thick branches.

Dark is the lantern's base while the light streams from above.

Don't jump into the fire with a bundle of wood.

Having enquired seven times, believe the common report.

Love leaves with the red petty coat.

Talk of a person and his shadow appears.

The mouth (i. e., greediness) is the door of all disease.

If in a hurry go round. The more hurry the less speed.

The spawn of frogs will become only frogs.

The walls have ears.

Pitchers have spouts.

Deaf men speak loud.

You cannot make fast a nail in potato custard.

By searching the old learn the new.

A rat-catching cat hides her claws.

If you keep a tiger you will have nothing but trouble.

An ugly woman shuns the looking glass.

To aim a gun in the darkness is vain.

What is the good in the peeping of a blind man through the hedge.

A charred stick is easily kindled.

Who steals money is killed, who steals a country is a king.

If you do not enter the den of the tiger you cannot get her cubs.

In mending the horn he killed the ox.

The best thing in travelling is a companion, the best thing in the world is kindness.

Famous words are made of iron-scrapers.

Though the magnet attracts iron, it cannot attract stone.

The gods have their seat on the brow of the just man.

Poke a cane-bush, and the snake will crawl out.

Use the cane before you fall down.

Lust has no bottom.

The world is just as a man's heart makes it.

Send the child you love most on a journey.

If you hate any one, let him live.

A cur bravely barks at its own gate.

Excessive politeness becomes impolite.

Even the monkey sometimes falls from the tree.

Poverty cannot overtake diligence.

The heron can rise from water without stirring the mud.

Adapt the preaching to the hearer.

If you curse any one, look out for two graves.

Hearing is paradise, seeing is hell.

THE CHINESE.

The Chinaman is the trunk, and the Japanese is the branch. The Chinaman is solid, substantial, self-consciousness. The English in China told me that his conceit is immeasurable. On the contrary the Japanese is light, airy, courteous to a fault, joking, and tittering at every step. The Chinaman never laughs, or when he does laugh, he laughs as through cotton. As Carlyle would say it is a hollow, unreal, toothful performance, which you would fain avoid. The Japanese has a reasonable share of conceit also. But he is so impressionable, in ancient and modern times he has been so intensely influenced by foreigners, that he unconsciously compares his stature with that of the world, and is abashed and humbled. The Chinaman is so stolid, so unperceiving, so absolutely without susceptibility that no comparison between him and the rest of mankind suggests itself, and he quietly sets them down as his inferiors. English trade, European civilization, the politics and diplomacy of the world impress the Chinaman with a supreme sense of his own importance, because he is making money for himself out of all these. The celestial is absolutely sold to the lust of lucre. He contemplates the whole universe through one midium, and that is the dollar. Coming suddenly from Japan to China is like a transit from some Rhenish islet to the troubled and turbid waters of the German Ocean. What an immense, surging, uncouth, unclean population is this! It is however a more vigorous, more promising, more fervid population. They have a character, they have a history, they have inviolable prejudices. Inviolable prejudices are almost always an element of strength. Up to this time, all the coaxing, all the finesse, all the bullying of English statesmanship have not persuaded the Chinese to allow an inch of railroad into their country. As for telegraphs they are out of the question. The European missionaries, nay even European military officers have to adopt the Chinese costume, shave their heads, and cultivate the pigtail to be able to have any influence with the people. But on the other hand the Japanese have begun to clothe their whole nation in tight trousers, porkpie hats, and green spectacles ! The Chinese woman keeps the Zenana, nay the condition of her feet makes it physically impossible for her to walk. In the very teeth of all this invading foreign civilization the Chinese sell and eat dried frogs, dried rats, and nameless other abominations. The Chinaman is an incomprehensible being. Observation proves that he is tame, mild, and yielding. Yet the French are finding at Tonquin that this immobility is not to be mistaken for cowardice or harmlessness. The Chinese have a great reverence for literature. Every body knows that long before the art of printing was dreamt of in Europe, in China they had wooden types from which they took delicate impressions. They were the first to manufacture paper, and no country in the world can excel the Chinese in the fineness and tissue of their paper manufacture. A thousand years before the birth of Christ they had invented, and were using the mariner's compass. Their written history dates back to something like twenty-six hundred years before the Christian era. The Chinaman therefore honors learning almost superstitiously. No paper with any writing on it can be used for packing, or any unworthy purpose. There are men going about with the avowed object of gathering inscribed waste paper. When a quantity is picked up it is respectfully committed to the flames like the remains of ancestors. Everybody knows what an involved and unique performance Chinese writing is. It is always executed with a brush, no pen is used. A Chinese book begins where our book ends. It is written from top to bottom the lines traversing to the left. There are three kinds of writing, the vulgar, the academic, and the sacred or sublime. The first is for business; the second for learning; the third is an object of veneration, the holy books of Confucius and Mencius are written in it. Each letter is the symbol of an idea, for there is no alphabet in China. And the symbols are combined and bound up to indicate a corresponding arrangement of ideas. Hence the writing is hieroglyphic. The spoken language is so difficult that the people of one province cannot without an interpreter understand the people of another province.

There is wonderful religious tolerance in China. In fact religious persecution is unknown. And whenever we hear of persecution, it arises from an attempt to influence politics through religion. The Christian missionaries are allowed to preach and convert in the heart of China. There are myriads of Mahomedans in China. There is a considerable number of Jews, and Buddhism always found a ready field for propagation there. The Chinaman will not permit social reform of any kind, no change in dress, customs, and established ways. But a man may profess and adopt any religion he likes. Some maintain that this is on account of the inveterate indifference of the Chinese for anything beyond the concerns of this life. If the Brahmo Somaj could master the difficulty of language, I have no doubt our missionaries could considerably influence the people. The Nestorians so early as 1330 are said to have converted 30,000 men. The Protestant missions which began so late as 1807 have about 5,600 converts. Between the followers of Buddha, Confucius, and Laotse there is no ill-feeling. The Chinese say " the three religions are one."

Abbe Huc, a famous writer on China says that when a number of men meet, the question first asked is "to what sublime religion may you belong." One will say he is a Buddhist; another that he is a Confucian; a third that he is a Mahomedan; the fourth that he is a Christian. Then every one begins to pronounce a panegyric on the religion to which he does not belong, as politeness requires. After which they all repeat in a chorus *Pou-toun Kias toun-ly*. Religions are many; reason is one; we are all brothers. Such is toleration in China.

When you reflect upon the mild Chinese look, it is difficult to think that they are a very cruel people. But their modes of execution, their forms of ordinary punishment for crime are horrible. Torture is a recognised and universal method of police investigation. The peace of Hong Kong is principally kept by a detachment of Sikh soldiers. But the Chinese policemen, called Lokungs, are there also, strangely dressed men, with umbrellas for hats, and immense gaiters and heavy batons. The bamboo tree flourishes in China. It not only serves every personal, social, and domestic purpose, but is the universal corrective of moral character. The father applies the bamboo on the undutiful offspring. The schoolmaster infuses literature by its aid into the mind of the scholar. The master enforces obedience on the servant with the bamboo. The Emperor applies bamboo on the naked skin of high officials to cure them of bribery. The magistrate makes unsparing use of it upon the plaintiff and defendant alike. Besides that, there is the *Cangue or Kia*. This is a heavy wooden square board, with a hole, into which the head is fitted closely, so that the whole thing forms a huge collar, about 50 pounds in weight. The criminal has his neck thrust into this apparatus, and locked up in it. He is to carry it day and night, and is not allowed to live in a habitation. His crime and the duration of his punishment are inscribed on the board. Whilst in the *Cangue* the man cannot reach his mouth with his hand, or see the rest of his body. He is made to sit at the gates of temples, and at other public places. Not a few die of the pain, shame, suffering, and want of rest.

Those who survive it are at the end of their term dismissed with a parting administration of 15 or 16 blows of the bamboo. Besides this, there are the punishments of finger-compressing, knee-squeezing, ear-twisting, and filling the eyes with quick-lime. In cases of capital punishment, men have their limbs cut away one after another, sometimes their bowels ripped open, and their hearts torn out and thrust upon their faces. The cruelty of Chinese punishment has become proverbial in the world. This is redeemed by the scrupulous regard the Chinese authorities pay to the management of their jails. Every death that occurs has to be accounted for in detail. The Emperor himself takes notice of deaths in prison. The position of the Emperor is simply divine. He is the father, mother, priest, and intercessor of the people. His private life is daily reported in the Pekin Gazette. His words, witticisms, blessings, wishes, are all described in full. They prostrate themselves in the dust before him, they call him the Son of Heaven. Rebellion against him is the deadliest of all crimes. The whole political, social and domestic organization of China turns upon the authority of the Emperor. Both the Japanese and Chinese eat not with their fingers, but with chop-sticks. As skilfully as the surgeon holds his lancet, the musician holds his drum-stick, the astronomer holds his telescope, the Chinaman holds his chop-sticks. With a professional unconcern, but rigid accuracy, he holds the two pieces of wood or bone. He holds them horizontally, perpendicularly, with one finger or two, and shoots his food into his mouth. The food is eaten in a bowl, never in a plate, and the bowl is lifted close to the mouth with the left hand, while the right holds the chop-sticks. Fish, pork, vegetable, lumps of rice are speared promiscuously, and hurled pell-mell without sound or ceremony into that omnivorous cavern from whose bourne no substance solid or liquid ever returns. Both in China and Japan they drink the rice-wine called *Saki*. In Japan they don't smoke opium. But in China opium-smoking and gambling form the first elements of human nature. Though there have been imperial edicts against both, the habit prevails in full force as ever before. The very women and children gamble. They gamble not only over cards, chess, and dice of course, but over everything. They spin tops, toss up copper coins, fight cocks, fight grasshoppers and crickets, and in every such mean frolic stake their miserable pittances. They gamble away their money, their clothes, their houses, their wives, and it is said sometimes even their fingers. which are chopped off when they lose the game. It is held that the Chinese were the first to make playing cards. A wonderful feature of Chinese life is the immense number of people who live in boats. Every sea-port or riverside city of China has its boat population. That of Canton alone numbers 300,000. They are born, they live and die on the curious-shaped boats some of which are from 20 to 30 feet deep. The women ply the oars and rudders with their tiny bright eyed babies strapped to their backs. They raise poultry, puppies, and kittens on their boats. They have theatres, concerts, acrobatic feats, tea-houses, and worse houses on boats. They make great rafts upon which they set up floating gardens, grow vegetables, and build residences that can be rented. Sometimes you see Chinese boats spreading over miles of water both in the river, and in the seas. The pirate junks of China were for a long time the dread of the seafaring world. Medical practice in China is very orthodox. They regard the beatings of the pulse with superstitious awe. How a disease originated, where its seat is, how soon it can be cured, everything can be ascertained from the pulse. If a doctor will promise to cure a patient, and fail, the relatives will hunt him out, sue him, beat him with bamboo, and make the place too hot for him to live in. If a patient is advanced in age, and an expensive drug is prescribed for him, he will be asked whether he would have the money spent on his cure, or on his coffin. Because, even if he is cured, being old he can not live long. Whereas, if the money is saved, he can have an ornamental coffin purchased. He often prefers the coffin to the cure!

PENANG AND SINGAPORE.

From Hong Kong to Singapore, the Chinese Sea is exceedingly shallow being less than fifty fathoms deep nearly all the way. The color of the water is faint green, and the coast lines of contiguous islands are pretty frequently seen. The weather grows more and more tropical every day, till reaching Singapore on the last day of December, we found the heat very distressing indeed. This was the time of the monsoon. The skies were heavily overcast, and as we were preparing to go on shore, showers broke out, continuing all day, and making our peregrinations most uncomfortable. The great feature of the island of Singapore is its immense vegetation. Our mental associations were still singed with the searness and nakedness of the November scenery of America. Now there burst forth before our gaze the profuse luxuriance of a vegetation which no spring I have experienced in any country could equal. Singapore is composed of a number of hills from three to four hundred feet high. To the very edge of water, where the sea laves their rocky basis, these hills are clothed in an exuberant vesture of intense green. High strange looking trees rear their stately crests, ferns and undergrowths fill up every patch of ground, palms and bananas of the most fantastic shapes stretch up their feathery arms, and the whole scenery has a freshness, brightness, and density belonging to virgin forests. But the dampness of the soil is something fearful. Whole tracts of jungle lay submerged in several inches of water. Everything had a soaked water-logged look. The streets wound through regular aisles of interlacing wood. Amidst the masses of this luxuriant verdure birds and parrots of all sizes, colors and kinds abound. Great cockatoos, immense green parrots, and red and mottled species of all kinds are brought for sale to the ships. Canes and bamboos of the most beautiful patterns are to be found in the bazar. Great wildernesses of cocoanut trees fill the horizon. The climate is never cold, nor is it any time excessively hot. Eternal spring has here its abode. A deep home-sickness siezes the mind as one beholds these familiar trees. The people too look familiar. The Madrasees, mostly called Klings, have emigrated into the Malay peninsula very extensively. They are the shopkeepers, hack-dealers, and hawkers of every description. You here and there meet with the sable Chettiars with their bored ears, bare backs, and stripes of white paint on the forehead. The Chinese live here by the thousand, with their dingy joss-houses, tawdry theatres, dirty eating-booths. And there is a handful of Parsees also. The European population cannot exceed a few thousands. The Malays themselves are mostly Mahomedans, boatmen, fishermen, and some of them shopkeepers. They are generally a fine-looking race, with a good deal of tall sturdy physique. Some of the women are quite delicate in appearance. Although we saw some boys returning from school, it does not seem that education or civilization has made much progress in Singapore and Penang. The people have just learnt to make a little money in a decent way, and commenced to live in better houses and better style than before. The missionaries are the only people who care for their welfare. And some of those missionaries are quite apostolical in their ways. When the people are in want, either bodily or mental, they go to their missionary father. They say "we have no rice in the house," and he immediately gives them half of what he has got. And when he wants any thing, he goes to them, and they give him his needs in coin, and in kind. I have come across a good many of these excellent missionaries in my travels over the Pacific. They go about with their families and children. I met them going to different parts of Japan and China, some to Formossa, some to Yesso, every one full of hope, faith, and earnestness. They cannot but do a great deal of good where they go, moral, religious, social, and every other kind of good work. Those I met were mostly Americans. And simple earnest philanthropic men and women they were. There were young ladies as missionary homœopaths, youngmen as medical propagandists. Some of them were quite liberal in their views and tendencies. They would most cheerfully co-operate with us if they got any opportunity. God bless them and their work in every way.

We had distant views of the islands of Borneo and Sumatra. Only a few miles from

Singapore are the territories of the Maharajah of Johore, who has lately travelled extensively in China and Japan. I followed with a good deal of interest the narrative of the doings of Sir James Brooke, otherwise called Rajah Brooke of Sarawak in Borneo. He had done his very best to civilize and educate the Dyaks and Malays under him. He invited missionaries and scientific men to visit and sojourn in Sarawak. He was most hospitable to them. The people found in him a guardian and father. He found them unprotected, lawless, poor. He left them settled in prosperity, blessed with fixed laws, well protected, and well known to all the world. But nothing in their estimation can compensate for his loss. Rajah Brook was a king, a legislator, a missionary, and an educationist at the same time. A few more Englishmen like him would do a great deal to reclaim and elevate the Malay races some of whom are said to be still very barbarous. There must have been at one time great prevalence of Hinduism in these islands. The names of places, the names of deities, and various words in the Malay language prove that the image of Durga, the ten-handed goddess, has been found in Borneo. And the traditions about her correspond almost exactly to what the people of Bengal believe. It is said that these islands at one time must have formed a part of the main land of Asia.

[Left Calcutta March 12th, and Arrived in London April 19th Thursday, 1883.]

TABLE OF OPERATIONS IN ENGLAND.

Dates.		Places.	Subjects of sermon and lecture.
Sunday April 22nd.		Stepney, London.	Divine Existence.
Wednesday April 25th.		Islington, do.	Religious out-look in India.
Sunday April 29th.	Morn. Even.	Stamford St. Stepney, } do.	The City of God. Prayer.
Wednesday May 2nd.		Exeter Hall, do.	Opium Traffic in India.
Sunday May 6th.	Morn. Even.	Portland St. Bermondsey Town Hall, } do.	Religion and Philosophy. Religious Opinion and Life in India.
Sunday May 13th.	Morn. Even.	Old Meeting, Bermingham.	Union with God. The Brahmo Somaj.
Wednesday May 16th.		Canon St. Hotel, London.	The Present Situation in the Brahmo Somaj.
Sunday May 20th.	Morn. Even.	Croydon, Surrey Peccam Rye, } do.	Sonship. Origin and Nature of Evil.
Sunday May 27th.	Morn. Even.	Roslyn Chapel Hampstead. Stratford } do.	The Dispensation of the Spirit. Atonement for Sin.

(212)

Dates.		Places.	Subjects &c.
Friday June 1st		Memorial Hall, Farringdon St. London.	The Development of the **B. S.**
Sunday June 3rd.		Did not preach—Spent the day at Oxford, and heard the University Sermon.	
Sunday June 10th	Morn. Even.	Masonic Hall } Bermingham do.	Sin and Salvation. Fruits of Monotheism.
Saturday June 16th.		Junior Liberal Club, do.	British Rule in India.
Sunday June 17th.	Morn. Even.	Church of the Messia } do. Town Hall	Prayer. Development of the B. S.
Friday June 22nd.		Manchester.	Religious Life.
Sunday June 24th.		Do.	History of the B. S.
Tuesday June 26th. Wednesday June 27th. Thursday June 28th.		The Lake districts.	Commn. with Nature, Meditation and Prayer.
Sunday July 1st.	Morn. Even.	Stockton on Tees	Providence. The New Dispensation.
Sunday July 8th.	Morn. Even.	New Castle on Tyne	The Dispensation of the Spirit. The Social work of the B. S.

Dates.	Places.	Subjects &c.
Thursday July 12th.	Kinnaird Hall, Dundee, Scotland.	Religion in India
Sunday July 15th.	Do.	The Order of Dispensations.
Wednesday July 18th.	Glasgow, Scotland	The Work of the B. S.
Friday July 20th.	Belfast, Ireland	Aims of the B. S.
Sunday July 22nd. Morn.	Presbyterian House, Belfast, Ireland.	Prayer.
Do. Even.	Money Rae	Attributes of God.
Tuesday July 24th.	Belfast	The Prospects of Indian Society
Sunday July 29th. Morn.	Liverpool	Future Life.
Even.	Manchester	Do.
Sunday August 5th.	Did not preach—Heard Mr. Stopford Brooke and Canon Liddon, London,	
Sunday August 12th.	Liverpool	Farewell Sermon on the New Dispensation.
Wednesday August 15th.	Left England for America.	

[Reached Boston, Tuesday, August 28th.]

TABLE OF OPERATIONS IN AMERICA.

Dates.	Places.	Subjects &c.
Sunday September 2nd.	Concord, Mass.	Rise and Development of the B. S.
Tuesday Sept. 4th	Social Science Association meetings Saratoga	[On the whole two speeches each day.] Religious life in India, Indian Races. The B. S. and such other subjects.
Wednesday „ 5th.		
Thursday „ 6th.		
Sunday Sept, 16th.	Boston [Congregational Church]	The Sympathy of Religions.
Saturday „ 22nd.	Wellesley (near Boston)	Speech on India to 500 young ladies of the Wellesley College.
Sunday „ 24th.	Boston [Ch. of Disciples, Unitarian]	The New Dispensation.
Wednesday „ 26th.	Lowel [Ministers' Institution]	Protestantism in India.
Thursday „ 27th.	Wellesley	Contemplation and Prayer in the woods.
Friday „ 28th.		
Sunday „ 30th,	New Port, nd. Island	What is God ?

(214)

Dates.		Places.	Subjects &c.
Thursday Oct 4th.		Hotel Vendome, Boston.	Reception and speech, Religion in India.
Sunday Oct 7th.	Morn.	Cambridge. Mass.	Yoga and Bhakti.
	Even.	Boston.	The New Dispensation.
Wednesday Oct 10th.	Morn.	Canton Mass. Hotel Vendome [Unitn. Club Dinner]	Simple Religion.
	Even.		Religious Unity.
Sunday Oct. 14th	Morn.	Hartford Conn.	Sermon and Aryan Monotheism.
	Even.	Congregational church do.	Social Reformation in the B. S.
Tuesday Oct. 16th		[Historical Society.] Brooklyn.	Hist. of Rational Religion in India.
Thursday Oct. 18th		Washington.	Hist of the B. S,
Sunday Oct. 21st		Brooklyn.	Three Periods in the B. S.
Wednesday Oct 24th		New York (Methodist) Ch.	Religion in India.
Thursday Oct. 25th		New York (Congregational) church.	The Brahmo Somaj.
Sunday Oct. 28th	Morn.	[Unitarian] church	Essential Religion.
	Even.	Do. New York	The Religion of the B. S.
Tuesday Oct. 30th		Brooklyn (Episcopal) Chr.	Reforms in the B. S.

(216)

Dates.		Places.	Subjects &c.
Sunday Nov. 4th.		Brooklyn. [Henry W. Beecher's Chapel.]	The New Dispensation.
Tuesday Nov 6th		Buffalo.	Religion in India.
Sunday Nov. 11th.	Morn.	(Unitarian.) Chicago.	The Order of Dispensations.
	Even.	(Congregational). Do.	History of the B. S.
Sunday Nov. 18th.	Morn.	San Francisco.	Unity of Religions.
	Even.		Social Work of the B. S.
Tuesday Nov. 22nd		Oaklands. (Near S. Francisco.)	India and the B. S.

Left America for Japan on Thursday the 24th November.

Reached Japan on Wednesday night, the 12th December.

Friday Dec. 14th.		Tokio. (University Hall).	Revived Budhism in the Brahmo-Somaj.
,, Dec. 21st.		Hongkong.	Visits to the Governor, Bishop, and others.

TABLE OF DISTANCES TRAVELLED.

	Miles.
Calcutta to Madras	770
Madras to Colombo	610
Colombo to Aden	2,093
Aden to Suez	1,308
The Canal	87
Portsaid to Alexandria	155
Alexandria to Malta	1,285
Malta to Gibralter	981
Gibralter to Plymouth	1,054
Plymouth to London	295
	8,638
Travels in England, Scotland, and Ireland about	1,700
Liverpool to Boston	2,850
Boston to San Francisco	3,500
Additional Travels in America	700
Fransisco to Yokohama	5,200
Yokohama to Hongkong	1,600
Honkong to Singapore	1,472
Singapore to Penang	381
Penang to Colombo	1,278
Colombo to Madras	610
Madras to Calcutta	770
	20,061
	8,638
	28,699
By Land	4,900
By Sea	23,799

ERRATA.

Page	Line	For	Read
17	2	George	John
,,	5	capucines	capuchins
19	9	outcaste	outcast
22	6	come	com-
24	19	swirling	whirling
29	1	was	is
36	16	and	*omit* and
48	5	tottertng	tottering
50	5	from	*omit* from
51	11	honey, moon	honey-moon
,,	13	hemesphere	hemisphere
54	7	270 averaging	averaging 270
55	2	somthing	something
57	11	cannat	cannot
61	14	Philadephia	Philadelphia
70	13	previlege	privilege
73	22	and	*omit* and
74	6	telectual	tellectual
,,	12	is great	is a great
,,	14	revolu-	resolu-

Page	Line	For	Read
75	23	Bud	But
77	15	hynms	hymns
,,	17	spunk	spun
78	18	thety	piety
,,	24	success yet the	success. The
80	2	men	man
87	9	height 160	height of 160
89	7	about quarter	about a quarter
92	17	it	its
96	14	furtile	fertile
99	13	It	If
103	2	actually swallow	actually to swallow
103	12	philsophy	philosophy
,,	20	Americans	the Americans
108	19	aqaintances	quaintance
126	13	country	county
137	14	courteseys	courtesies
138	18	sowly	slowly
145	15	your's	yours
157	24	lobours	labours
159	18	mostached	mustached
211	3rd col. 16	Sonshrip	Sonship

www.ingramcontent.com/pod-product-compliance
Lightning Source LLC
LaVergne TN
LVHW061213060426
835507LV00016B/1911